2018 SQA Past Papers with Answers

National 5
ENGLISH

2016, 2017 & 2018 Exams

National 5 ENGLISH

HODDER
GIBSON
AN HACHETTE UK COMPANY

This book contains the official SQA 2016, 2017 and 2018 Exams for National 5 English, with associated SQA-approved answers modified from the official marking instructions that accompany the paper.

In addition the book contains study skills advice. This advice has been specially commissioned by Hodder Gibson, and has been written by experienced senior teachers and examiners in line with the new National 5 syllabus and assessment outlines. This is not SQA material but has been devised to provide further guidance for National 5 examinations.

Hodder Gibson is grateful to the copyright holders, as credited on the final page of the Answer section, for permission to use their material. Every effort has been made to trace the copyright holders and to obtain their permission for the use of copyright material. Hodder Gibson will be happy to receive information allowing us to rectify any error or omission in future editions.

Hachette UK's policy is to use papers that are natural, renewable and recyclable products and made from wood grown in sustainable forests. The logging and manufacturing processes are expected to conform to the environmental regulations of the country of origin.

Orders: please contact Bookpoint Ltd, 130 Park Drive, Milton Park, Abingdon, Oxon OX14 4SE. Telephone: (44) 01235 827827. Fax: (44) 01235 400454. Lines are open 9.00–5.00, Monday to Saturday, with a 24-hour message answering service. Visit our website at www.hoddereducation.co.uk. Hodder Gibson can also be contacted directly at hoddergibson@hodder.co.uk

This collection first published in 2018 by
Hodder Gibson, an imprint of Hodder Education,
An Hachette UK Company
211 St Vincent Street
Glasgow G2 5QY

Typeset by Aptara, Inc.

Printed in the UK

A catalogue record for this title is available from the British Library

ISBN: 978-1-5104-5595-5

2 1

2019 2018

Introduction

National 5 English

The course specifications for National 5 English changed in 2017 and Units and Unit Assessments were removed. The 2017 and 2018 Past Papers reflect this, and the 2016 paper remains an incredibly useful revision tool. The questions contained in this book provide excellent representative exam practice.

Your teacher will advise you on preparation for the ongoing *Portfolio* and *Performance* elements of your assessment. Using these past papers as part of your revision will help you to learn the vital skills and techniques needed for the *Reading for Understanding, Analysis and Evaluation* and *Critical Reading* papers, and identify any knowledge gaps you may have, prior to the exam season in May–June.

It is always a very good idea to refer to SQA's website for the most up-to-date course specification documents. These are available at https://www.sqa.org.uk/sqa/47410

The course

The National 5 English course aims to enable you to develop the ability to:

- Listen, talk, read and write, as appropriate to purpose, audience and context
- Understand, analyse and evaluate texts, including Scottish texts, in the contexts of literature, language and/or the media
- Create and produce texts, as appropriate to purpose, audience and context, through the application of your knowledge and understanding of language.

How the course is graded

The grade you finally get for National 5 English depends on three things:

- The Performance – Spoken Language component, which is assessed in your school or college; this doesn't count towards your final grade, but you must have achieved the minimum requirements in it before you can get a final graded award.
- Your Portfolio of Writing – this is submitted in April for marking by SQA and counts for 30% of your final grade.
- The two exams you sit in May – that's what this book is all about.

The exams

Reading for Understanding, Analysis and Evaluation

- exam time: 1 hour
- total marks: 30
- weighting in final grade: 30%
- what you have to do: read a passage and answer questions about it.

Critical Reading

- exam time: 1 hour 30 minutes
- total marks: 40 (20 for each section)
- weighting in final grade: 40%
- what you have to do: (Section 1) read an extract from one of the Scottish Texts which are set for National 5 and answer questions about it; (Section 2) write an essay about a work of literature you have studied during your course.

Reading for Understanding, Analysis and Evaluation

Three important tips to start with

- Since there will usually be a question asking you to summarise some or all of the passage, it is really important to read the whole passage before you even look at the questions. Doing this will give you a chance to get a rough idea of the main ideas in the passage, and you can add to this as you work your way through the questions.
- Pay close attention to the number of marks available for each question and make sure your answer is appropriate to the number of marks. In questions about understanding, you will get 1 mark for each correct point; in questions about language features, you will get 1 mark for an appropriate quotation from the text and 1 mark for a sensible comment on the quotation.
- Some questions tell you to "use your own words". This means you mustn't just copy chunks from the passage – you have to show that you understand what it means by rephrasing it in your own words.

Questions which ask for understanding

- Keep your answers fairly short and pay attention to the number of marks available.

Questions about language features

- This type of question will ask you to comment on features such as word choice, imagery, sentence structure and tone.
- You should pick out a relevant language feature and make a valid comment about its impact. Try to make your comments as specific as possible and avoid vague comments (like "It is a good word to use because it gives me a clear picture of what the writer is saying").

- Some hints:
  - **Word choice:** Always try to pick a single word or expression and then give its connotations, i.e. what it **suggests**.
  - **Sentence structure:** Don't just name the feature – try to explain what effect it achieves **in that particular sentence**.
  - **Imagery:** Try to explain what the image means **literally** and then go on to explain what the writer is **suggesting** by using that image.
  - **Tone:** This is always difficult – a good tip is to imagine the sentence or paragraph being read out loud and try to spot how the words or the structure give it a particular tone.

Summary questions

- Make sure you follow the instruction about what it is you are to summarise (the question will be as helpful as possible).
- Stick to the main ideas; avoid unimportant points and never include examples.
- Make sure you earn all the marks available for the question.

Critical Reading

Section 1 – Scottish Text

The most important thing to remember here is that there are two very different types of question to be answered:

- Three or four questions (for a total of 12 marks) which focus entirely on the extract.
- One question (for 8 marks) which requires knowledge of the whole text (or of another poem or short story by the same writer).

The first type of question will often ask you to use the same close reading skills you use in the RUAE part of the exam, such as summary of key points and analysis of word choice, imagery and sentence structure. The golden rule, however, is always to read each question very carefully and do exactly as instructed.

The last question, for 8 marks, can be answered **either** in bullet points **or** as a "mini essay". Choose whichever approach you are more comfortable with. Make as many relevant points as you can. If you look at the Marking Guide which is used for this type of question (see page 123), you'll get an idea of how this question is marked and this should help you in your approach.

Final bit of advice for the Scottish Text question: when you see the extract in the exam paper, don't get too confident just because you recognise it (you certainly should recognise it if you've studied properly!). And even if you've answered questions on it before, remember that the questions in the exam are likely to be different, so stay alert.

Section 2 – Critical Essay

A common mistake is to rely too heavily on ideas and whole paragraphs you have used in practice essays and try to use them for the question you have chosen in the exam. The trick is to come to the exam with lots of ideas and thoughts about at least one of the texts you have studied and use these to tackle the question you choose from the exam paper. You mustn't use the exam question as an excuse to trot out an answer you've prepared in advance.

Structure

Every good essay has a structure, but there is no "correct" structure, no magic formula that the examiners are looking for. It's **your** essay, so structure it the way **you** want. As long as you're answering the question all the way through, then you'll be fine.

Relevance

Be relevant to the question **all the time** – not just in the first and last paragraphs.

Central concerns

Try to make sure your essay shows that you have thought about and understood the central concerns of the text, i.e. what it's "about" – the ideas and themes the writer is exploring in the text.

Quotations

In poetry and drama essays, you're expected to quote from the text, but never fall into the trap of learning a handful of quotations and forcing them all into the essay regardless of the question you're answering. In prose essays, quotation is much less important, and you can show your knowledge much more effectively by referring in detail to what happens in key sections of the novel or the short story.

Techniques

You are expected to show some understanding of how various literary techniques work within a text, but simply naming them will not get you marks, and structuring your essay around techniques rather than around relevant ideas in the text is not a good idea.

Good luck!

Remember that the rewards for passing National 5 English are well worth it! Your pass will help you get the future you want for yourself. In the exam, be confident in your own ability. If you're not sure how to answer a question, trust your instincts and just give it a go anyway – keep calm and don't panic! GOOD LUCK!

Study Skills – what you need to know to pass exams!

General exam revision: 20 top tips

When preparing for exams, it is easy to feel unsure of where to start or how to revise. This guide to general exam revision provides a good starting place, and, as these are very general tips, they can be applied to all your exams.

1. Start revising in good time.

Don't leave revision until the last minute – this will make you panic and it will be difficult to learn. Make a revision timetable that counts down the weeks to go.

2. Work to a study plan.

Set up sessions of work spread through the weeks ahead. Make sure each session has a focus and a clear purpose. What will you study, when and why? Be realistic about what you can achieve in each session, and don't be afraid to adjust your plans as needed.

3. Make sure you know exactly when your exams are.

Get your exam dates from the SQA website and use the timetable builder tool to create your own exam schedule. You will also get a personalised timetable from your school, but this might not be until close to the exam period.

4. Make sure that you know the topics that make up each course.

Studying is easier if material is in manageable chunks – why not use the SQA topic headings or create your own from your class notes? Ask your teacher for help on this if you are not sure.

5. Break the chunks up into even smaller bits.

The small chunks should be easier to cope with. Remember that they fit together to make larger ideas. Even the process of chunking down will help!

6. Ask yourself these key questions for each course:

- Are all topics compulsory or are there choices?
- Which topics seem to come up time and time again?
- Which topics are your strongest and which are your weakest?

Use your answers to these questions to work out how much time you will need to spend revising each topic.

7. Make sure you know what to expect in the exam.

The subject-specific introduction to this book will help with this. Make sure you can answer these questions:

- How is the paper structured?
- How much time is there for each part of the exam?
- What types of question are involved? These will vary depending on the subject so read the subject-specific section carefully.

8. Past papers are a vital revision tool!

Use past papers to support your revision wherever possible. This book contains the answers and mark schemes too – refer to these carefully when checking your work. Using the mark scheme is useful; even if you don't manage to get all the marks available first time when you first practise, it helps you identify how to extend and develop your answers to get more marks next time – and of course, in the real exam.

9. Use study methods that work well for you.

People study and learn in different ways. Reading and looking at diagrams suits some students. Others prefer to listen and hear material – what about reading out loud or getting a friend or family member to do this for you? You could also record and play back material.

10. There are three tried and tested ways to make material stick in your long-term memory:

- Practising – e.g. rehearsal, repeating
- Organising – e.g. making drawings, lists, diagrams, tables, memory aids
- Elaborating – e.g. incorporating the material into a story or an imagined journey

11. Learn actively.

Most people prefer to learn actively – for example, making notes, highlighting, redrawing and redrafting, making up memory aids, or writing past paper answers. A good way to stay engaged and inspired is to mix and match these methods – find the combination that best suits you. This is likely to vary depending on the topic or subject.

12. Be an expert.

Be sure to have a few areas in which you feel you are an expert. This often works because at least some of them will come up, which can boost confidence.

13. Try some visual methods.

Use symbols, diagrams, charts, flashcards, post-it notes etc. Don't forget – the brain takes in chunked images more easily than loads of text.

14. Remember – practice makes perfect.

Work on difficult areas again and again. Look and read – then test yourself. You cannot do this too much.

15. Try past papers against the clock.

Practise writing answers in a set time. This is a good habit from the start but is especially important when you get closer to exam time.

16. Collaborate with friends.

Test each other and talk about the material – this can really help. Two brains are better than one! It is amazing how talking about a problem can help you solve it.

17. Know your weaknesses.

Ask your teacher for help to identify what you don't know. Try to do this as early as possible. If you are having trouble, it is probably with a difficult topic, so your teacher will already be aware of this – most students will find it tough.

18. Have your materials organised and ready.

Know what is needed for each exam:

- Do you need a calculator or a ruler?
- Should you have pencils as well as pens?
- Will you need water or paper tissues?

19. Make full use of school resources.

Find out what support is on offer:

- Are there study classes available?
- When is the library open?
- When is the best time to ask for extra help?
- Can you borrow textbooks, study guides, past papers, etc.?
- Is school open for Easter revision?

20. Keep fit and healthy!

Try to stick to a routine as much as possible, including with sleep. If you are tired, sluggish or dehydrated, it is difficult to see how concentration is even possible. Combine study with relaxation, drink plenty of water, eat sensibly, and get fresh air and exercise – all these things will help more than you could imagine. Good luck!

NATIONAL 5

2016

National Qualifications 2016

X724/75/11

**English
Reading for Understanding,
Analysis and Evaluation**

THURSDAY, 5 MAY

1:00 PM — 2:00 PM

Total marks — 30

Attempt ALL questions.

Write your answers clearly in the answer booklet provided. In the answer booklet you must clearly identify the question number you are attempting.

Use **blue** or **black** ink.

Before leaving the examination room you must give your answer booklet to the Invigilator; if you do not, you may lose all the marks for this paper.

Can Idina Menzel ever Let It Go?

When the organisers of the 2015 Super Bowl were looking for someone to follow in the footsteps of Diana Ross and Whitney Houston and belt out *The Star-Spangled Banner* in front of a global audience of 160 million, it's not hard to see why they chose Idina Menzel.

5   As the voice of Elsa the ice queen in *Frozen*, the most successful animated film of all time, who sang its ubiquitous Oscar-winning *Let It Go* (more than three million copies sold in America alone), she has a more than passing acquaintance with anthems.

The stratospheric success of *Frozen* — with takings of more than £800 million, it's No 5 in the all-time list of highest-grossing films — has elevated her into a new league.

Now she releases hit Christmas albums, has Broadway shows written for her, tours the
10   world's mega-domes and is having a TV sitcom developed.

Frozen isn't going away, either. She's spoken in the past about the much-mooted sequel but she has clearly been reprimanded by the Disney suits: "Apparently I spoke out of turn. I just assumed that because it was so successful there'd be a sequel, but Disney doesn't have sequels, so it would be a first if there was one."

15   How about the *Frozen* stage show, also much mooted? "I think they're working on that but the Disney people keep things close to their chests." If it happens, would she like to be in it? "Sure, I'd love to. But musicals take years and I'd have to play Elsa's mother, probably!"

What's definitely happening is a six-minute short, *Frozen Fever*, in which Elsa's powers threaten to scupper the birthday of her sister, Anna. "It's fun, really clever," Menzel says.
20   "There's a new song. It's pretty much a group number though." She sounds slightly disappointed.

Frozen Fever did delight both fans and Disney — it was shown in cinemas before Disney's live-action *Cinderella*, which doubtless enjoyed a mighty bump as a result. The studio may be tight-lipped about *Frozen* sequels, but they're certainly happy to milk the
25   commercial opportunities of their icy behemoth.

Whether there is a *Frozen 2* or not, Menzel is now a big star, there to be shot at. When she performed *Let It Go* in Times Square in New York on New Year's Eve she was criticised for failing to hit a high note (to be fair, she was singing in sub-zero temperatures). And though her powerful, stately turn at the Super Bowl received strong reviews, there were
30   still some who noticed the odd flat note.

The unnerving proximity of several dozen hulking American footballers may have had something to do with that. Talking about the time that she sang at the All-Star baseball game, Menzel says: "One thing I underestimated is what a strong presence these athletes have when they're standing on the line right in front of you. They're huge, standing
35   there, and you're this one woman, singing on her own. You forget about the world and the rest of the stadium because they're so . . . daunting."

One woman opposite a squad of men: it's a pertinent image given her associations with *Frozen*, a film that has regularly been touted as a feminist breakthrough. The first Disney animation to be directed (well, co-directed) by a woman, Jennifer Lee, it's quietly
40   revolutionary because, as Menzel says, "the purest love that's being celebrated is between two sisters and not because some Prince Charming is saving the day".

Yes, the two heroines are still doe-eyed and partial to shiny dresses, but their relationship is subtle: Elsa, the conflicted snow sorceress struggling to control her powers; Anna, the devoted younger sister whom she keeps at a distance for fear of turning her into a
45   popsicle. With her grandiose sulks, Elsa has been described as Disney's first emo princess. "She's definitely complicated," Menzel says. "I think that's why it's a successful film, because both women are not stereotypes."

50 There are parallels with Menzel's own life: she and her younger sister, Cara, had their fair share of "Do you wanna build a snowman?" moments. "She would probably tell you she looks up to me, a lot," Menzel says, rather wincingly.

When *Let It Go* was nominated for Best Song at the Oscars a year ago, it was Cara whom Menzel took as her date. "I didn't think about it — she was the first person I thought of — and then I realised how perfect it was," she says. Sisters representing a film about sisters.

55 *Let It Go* won the Oscar for its writers, but that was rather overshadowed by the moment of weirdness earlier in the evening when, introducing Menzel's performance of the song, John Travolta inexplicably referred to her as "Adele Dazeem".

60 She nevertheless recognises that Travolta's slip was "one of the greatest mistakes ever — it helped my career, that's for sure." It's one of several references Menzel makes to her career: her conversation is a mix of Broadway-speak ("I try to sing from the heart") and battle-hardened ambition.

65 She is certainly aware of the value of appearing in "several zeitgeist-y things across different generations: from *Rent* to *Wicked*, *Glee* to *Frozen*". There's a 'through line' between those four, she thinks: they all resonate with young people and "people who are trying to find themselves. I'm proud of that. I'm not sure why that's become the pattern for me — maybe it's because I have as much to learn myself".

Our time is almost up. I'm allowed to ask one more (burning) question. Does she have her own Elsa dress, the must-have wardrobe item for girls across the western world? "No I do not!" she laughs.

70 So she doesn't ever have the urge to indulge her inner ice queen and don the full regalia? "Nah, I don't look that good as a blonde. The waistline, though — that would be fun." Part of me suspects that she'd also quite enjoy ruling over her own wintry kingdom.

Ed Potton, in "The Times"

MARKS

Total marks — 30

Attempt ALL Questions

1. Look at lines 1–6, and then explain **in your own words** why the organisers of the Super Bowl chose Idina Menzel to perform there.

2

2. Look at lines 7–8, and then, by referring to **one** example, explain fully how the writer's use of language makes it clear that Frozen is successful.

2

3. Look at lines 11–25, and then identify, **using your own words** as far as possible, **five** things we learn here about the Disney organisation.

5

4. Look at lines 26–36, and then explain fully how the writer's use of language makes it clear that coping with performing under these circumstances is not easy. You should refer to **two** examples in your answer.

4

5. By referring to the sentence in lines 37–38, explain how it helps to provide a link between the writer's ideas at this point in the passage.

2

6. Look at lines 42–47, and then explain fully how **two** examples of the writer's **word choice** make it clear that Elsa is not just "doe-eyed and partial to shiny dresses".

4

7. Look at lines 51–61, and then explain fully **in your own words** as far as possible why the Oscar evening was so memorable or such a success for Idina Menzel.

2

8. Look at lines 62–69, by referring to **two** examples, explain fully how the writer makes effective use of contrast in these paragraphs. You could refer to sentence structure, tone or word choice.

4

9. Throughout the passage, we are given information and clues about Idina Menzel's personality.

    Using your own words as far as possible, identify **five** things that we learn about her personality from the passage.

5

[END OF QUESTION PAPER]

National Qualifications
2016

X724/75/12

English
Critical Reading

THURSDAY, 5 MAY

2:20 PM — 3:50 PM

Total marks — 40

SECTION 1 — Scottish Text — 20 marks

Read an extract from a Scottish text you have previously studied.

Choose ONE text from either

Part A — Drama   Pages 2—7

or

Part B — Prose   Pages 8—17

or

Part C — Poetry   Pages 18—25

Attempt ALL the questions for your chosen text.

SECTION 2 — Critical Essay — 20 marks

Attempt ONE question from the following genres — Drama, Prose, Poetry, Film and Television Drama, or Language.

Your answer must be on a different genre from that chosen in Section 1.

You should spend approximately 45 minutes on each Section.

Write your answers clearly in the answer booklet provided. In the answer booklet you must clearly identify the question number you are attempting.

Use **blue** or **black** ink.

Before leaving the examination room you must give your answer booklet to the Invigilator; if you do not, you may lose all the marks for this paper.

SECTION 1 — SCOTTISH TEXT — 20 marks

PART A — SCOTTISH TEXT — DRAMA

Text 1 — Drama

If you choose this text you may not attempt a question on Drama in Section 2.

Read the extract below and then attempt the following questions.

***Bold Girls* by Rona Munro**

Extract from Scene Four (Marie and Deirdre are in Marie's house . . .)

DEIRDRE: But you'd know. I know you'd look at me and you'd be sure.

Marie doesn't turn

Deirdre gets up and clumsily pulls off her top, drags off the jeans. There are bruises all over her back. She goes to Marie and pushes the clothes in front of
5 *her*

Here, that's you got everything back.

Marie turns, startled, then starts to laugh, hysterically. Deirdre hurls the clothes at her. She snatches the knife out of the chair and waves the blade at Marie. She advances on her slowly

10 I want the truth out of you. I mean it.

Marie backs off a step

Tell me!

Suddenly Marie flies at her

MARIE: Tell you! I'll tell you!

15 *She wrenches the knife and the picture off the startled Deirdre and smashes and slashes Michael's picture with swift, efficient destructiveness. She looks down at the pieces at her feet for a long moment. She drops the knife on top of them. Her breathing slows. She goes to the kitchen area and comes back with a half-filled rubbish sack and some newspaper. She kneels down and*
20 *starts to clear up the pieces of the picture*

(*Quietly*) Watch your feet on that glass there. (*She wraps the glass and the shredded picture in the newspaper. She wraps the knife as well. She drops both in the rubbish sack and takes it back to the kitchen*)

Deirdre has barely moved through all of this, she watches Marie tearfully

25 *Marie returns from the kitchen, wiping her hands*

(*Still quietly*) There. (*She looks at Deirdre*) Those are some bruises you've got.

Marie reaches out and touches Deirdre's shoulder

Deirdre flinches, then allows the touch

Marie turns her gently. She looks at her bruised body. Marie touches Deirdre's
30 *back*

MARKS

MARIE: Who did this to you?

DEIRDRE: Just the fella she's got living with her just now.

MARIE: (*Stroking Deirdre's back*) They took the lying head off Michael, didn't you know? Didn't they tell you that story?

35 DEIRDRE: (*Quietly*) Yes. (*She pulls away from Marie*)

              Marie seems to focus on her again

MARIE: Ah God forgive me . . . (*She sways momentarily. She runs her hands over her face*) You should go home. It's late.

              Deirdre doesn't move

40   Here. (*She offers the clothes again*)

              Deirdre shakes her head again

Questions

1. Using your own words as far as possible, summarise what happens in this extract. You should make **three** key points.   3

2. Look at the stage directions in lines 1—13.

    By referring to **two** examples, show how the playwright reveals that Marie is emotional in this part of the scene.   4

3. Look at lines 15—23.

    Identify **one** of Marie's actions and go on to explain in your own words why this action is surprising.   2

4. Think about Deirdre's attitude towards Marie in this extract.

    Identify any aspect of Deirdre's attitude and by referring to **one** example of her dialogue, explain fully how the playwright conveys this aspect of Deirdre's attitude towards Marie.   3

5. There are many examples of conflict in this play. By referring to this extract and to elsewhere in the play, show how conflict is an important feature of the play.   8

[**Turn over**

OR

Text 2 — Drama

If you choose this text you may not attempt a question on Drama in Section 2.

Read the extract below and then attempt the following questions.

Sailmaker **by Alan Spence**

	ALEC:	How come ye chucked yer trade?
	DAVIE:	It chucked me! The chandlers ah worked for shut doon. Ah got laid off. That was it. Nothin else doin. Nae work. Naebody needs sailmakers these days.
5	ALEC:	(*Holds up yacht*) Could ye make me a sail for this? Ah found it in the Glory Hole tae. Ah thought ye could fix it up.
	DAVIE:	Oh aye. It's a beauty, eh? Be nice, aw rigged out.
		Can sail it in the park.
		Course, it'll take time. Materials'll be dear. But ah'll see what ah can do.
	ALEC:	When?
10	DAVIE:	Wait and see. (*Hands back yacht*) Who knows? Maybe ma coupon'll come up this week!
	ALEC:	Remember the last time ye won?
	DAVIE:	First dividend. Two quid!
15		Ah didnae let it go tae ma head mind! Didnae chuck ma job. Didnae buy a villa in the south of France. Ah think every second game was a draw that week! Never mind. Some ae these days.
		(*DAVIE sits down, takes newspaper and scrap of paper from his briefcase, writes*)
		Ah didnae bring in anythin for tea. D'ye fancy nippin doon tae the chippy, gettin a coupla fish suppers?
20	ALEC:	Awright.
		(*DAVIE hands him money*)
		Can ah get a pickle?
	DAVIE:	Get anythin ye like. Here's somethin else ye can do for me.
		Themorra at dinnertime. Take this line to the bookie.
25	ALEC:	Och da!
	DAVIE:	Whit's the matter?
	ALEC:	It's just that . . . ah don't like that bookie. He's creepy.
	DAVIE:	Away ye go!
	ALEC:	An that back close where he has his pitch is aw horrible an smelly.

MARKS

30 DAVIE: (*Waves his line*) But this could be worth a fortune! Three doubles, a treble, an accumulator. If it comes up we're laughin.

Here son, ah'll leave it here wi the money inside it.

ALEC: (*Picks up line, reads it*) Why d'ye always write Mainsail at the bottom ae yer line?

35 DAVIE: That's what ye call a nom-de-plume. The bettin's illegal ye see. The bookie gets done fae time tae time. An if you put yer real name on the line, the polis might book you as well. So ye use a made-up name.

ALEC: Mainsail.

Questions

6. Using your own words as far as possible, explain how Davie is shown to be struggling in his role as a father throughout this extract. You should make **four** key points.   4

7. Look at lines 2—3 and lines 10—16.

By referring to **two** examples from these lines, show how different aspects of Davie's mood are revealed by the playwright.   4

8. Look at lines 33—38.

(a) Using your own words as far as possible, explain why Davie needed to use a false name (nom-de-plume).   2

(b) Explain what **two** things Davie's choice of false name (nom-de-plume) reveals about him.   2

9. By referring to this extract and to elsewhere in the play, show how the yacht is used as an important symbol.   8

[Turn over

OR

Text 3 — Drama

If you choose this text you may not attempt a question on Drama in Section 2.

Read the extract below and then attempt the following questions.

Tally's Blood by Ann Marie di Mambro

	BRIDGET:	I knew you'd try to split them up. I warned our Hughie, but I never knew the lengths you'd go to.
	ROSINELLA:	What you talking about?
5	BRIDGET:	You sent her back, didn't you? Didn't care who gets hurt. After all these years you sent her away.
	ROSINELLA:	Who?
	BRIDGET:	Lucia. Who else?
	ROSINELLA:	Send Lucia away? Me?
	BRIDGET:	Well, you did it to me, but you're no getting doing it to my brother.
10	ROSINELLA:	I don't want to hear any more. What did I ever do to you?
	BRIDGET:	What did you do to me? You told me Franco didn't love me. You made me believe I was nothing to him — just a wee Scottish tart for him to practise on.
	ROSINELLA:	In God's name, Bridget, that's all in the past.
15	BRIDGET:	To you maybe. But there's no a day goes past that it's no with me. Franco loved me. Franco loved me.
	ROSINELLA:	Franco's dead — and may God forgive you, lady, for dragging his name through the mud.
20		*This remark knocks BRIDGET off her guard and ROSINELLA gathers her strength.*
	ROSINELLA:	Now, I didn't want this fight with you, and I don't have to explain nothing to you. But just you hear this. I didn't send Lucia away, I could just as easily tear out my own heart. But I'm no sorry she's away from your brother. I cannie deny it. No harm to the boy. I've nothing against him. OK? Now that's it finished. We'll forget this conversation ever took place.
25		
	BRIDGET:	As easy as that.
	ROSINELLA:	Yes.
	BRIDGET:	All forgotten.
	ROSINELLA:	I'll never mention it again.
30	BRIDGET:	If you knew the damage you've caused.
	ROSINELLA:	(*Angry*) That's it. I've had enough. I don't have to stand here and listen to this. You think I'm not suffering? Lucia's more than a niece to me, more than somebody else's lassie that I brought up and grew to love. She's like the child I could never have.
35		*Silence: BRIDGET thinks, then decides.*

MARKS

BRIDGET:	The child you never had, eh, Mrs Pedreschi? What about the child I never had?	
ROSINELLA:	(*Dismissive*) What you going on about now?	
BRIDGET:	Do you remember that night, I came to see you? I was pregnant.	
40	*ROSINELLA shakes her head.*	
ROSINELLA:	What you saying?	
BRIDGET:	I was pregnant and it was Franco's baby.	
	ROSINELLA backs off in disbelief.	

Questions

10. Using your own words as far as possible, summarise what happens in the extract. You should make **four** key points.   4

11. Look at lines 11—16.

    Show how both word choice **and** sentence structure are used to reveal Bridget's feelings.   4

12. With reference to **two** examples from the extract show how Rosinella's attitude towards Bridget develops.   4

13. By referring to this extract and to elsewhere in the play, show how the playwright explores family relationships.   8

[Turn over

SECTION 1 — SCOTTISH TEXT — 20 marks

PART B — SCOTTISH TEXT — PROSE

Text 1 — Prose

If you choose this text you may not attempt a question on Prose in Section 2.

Read the extract below and then attempt the following questions.

The Cone-Gatherers by Robin Jenkins

In this extract, Roderick has decided to take some cake to the cone-gatherers, but encounters Duror in the wood.

Peeping through the yew needles, Roderick saw in imagination the door of the hut open, and the cone-gatherers come out, the tall one who slightly limped and always frowned, and the small one who stooped and smiled. Then in the cypress the gun cracked, and the two men lay dead on the grass.

5   It was while he was imagining Duror come stalking out to gloat over the corpses that the idea took root in the boy's mind that perhaps it was Duror himself who was dead. That idea sprouted. Duror had been strolling through the wood, had felt a pain at his heart, and had clutched at the cypress to keep from falling; there he had died, and the green bony arms were propping him up.

10   To Roderick, growing in a time of universal war, distant human death was a commonplace: he had listened to many wireless estimates of enemies killed and had loyally been pleased. Only once, when his grandfather died, had death appeared to him as a tyrant, snatching ruthlessly away what he loved, putting darkness and terror in its place, and at random moments, even in the middle of the night when the rest of the house slept, creating fragments of joy only to
15   annihilate them thereafter. Now the thought of Duror standing dead among the branches of the evergreen brought no hope, but rather began to infect the whole visible world with a sense of loss and desolation and fear. Every single leaf was polluted; even a tiny black beetle close to his head represented the vast tyranny. It was as if all the far off deaths he had rejoiced at were now gathering here around the yew trees to be revenged. Yet was not Duror
20   evil, and if evil died did not goodness triumph? Why then were all the birds not singing, and why did the sun not begin to shine again with morning splendour, and why, above all, was the hut now in shadow? Unable to answer those questions, the boy knelt in an unhappiness too profound and violent for tears or prayer; its only outward signs were paleness and the extra prominence of his teeth.

25   When at last, in the gloaming, Duror moved, it was to the stricken boy like a resurrection, darkening incomprehension and deepening despair. From the arms of the tree Duror stepped forth, and stood for a minute in the clearing in front of the hut. It was a minute of cessation. Incalculable in thought or feeling, gigantic in horror, as if indeed newly come from the dead, Duror merely stood. Then, without any interpretable gesture, and
30   without a sound, he turned and vanished among the trees, as if this time forever.

MARKS

Questions

14. Look at lines 1—9.

    Explain how the writer uses **two** examples of language in these lines to describe what Roderick imagines.

    4

15. Using your own words as far as possible, explain **two** different ways in which Roderick thinks of death in lines 10—19.

    2

16. Explain how the writer uses **two** examples of language to create a frightening atmosphere in lines 17—24.

    4

17. Look at the final sentence of the extract ("Then . . . forever."). By referring to **one** example of word choice, explain how the writer makes Duror's actions appear dramatic.

    2

18. With reference to the extract and to elsewhere in the novel, show how war is an important feature of the novel.

    8

[**Turn over**

OR

Text 2 — Prose

If you choose this text you may not attempt a question on Prose in Section 2.

Read the extract below and then attempt the following questions.

The Testament of Gideon Mack by James Robertson

The following extract is from the prologue. The editor has just described Gideon Mack's fall into the Black Jaws.

However, three days after this incident, while the community was still coming to terms with its loss, the body of Mr Mack was found washed up on the bank of the Keldo a short distance downstream of the Black Jaws. Not only had the water apparently carried him through its unknown course, but, even more amazingly, he was alive, and without a broken bone in his
5 body. True, he was badly battered, he had a large bruise on the side of his head, and his right leg had sustained some kind of internal damage which left him with a severe limp, but he had somehow survived three nights outdoors and a subterranean journey that no creature, except a fish, could have been expected to survive. He was taken to hospital in Dundee, where he remained unconscious but stable for a day and a half. When he came round he astonished
10 medical staff by making such a speedy recovery that less than a week after the accident he was discharged and sent home.

Back in Monimaskit, Mr Mack convalesced at his manse and seemed in no great hurry to resume his pastoral duties. It was at this time that he began to talk to some people of his experience. He claimed that he had been rescued from the river by a stranger, a man
15 inhabiting the caverns through which he said it passed, and that he had been looked after by this individual. This seemed improbable enough, but Mr Mack went on to assert that this person was none other than the Devil, and that they had had several long conversations in the course of the three days. These remarks were taken by the minister's friends as indication of a severe shock to his system, and possibly of damage to the brain
20 sustained during his ordeal. Others, however, were less concerned with his health than with the injury his words might do to the good name of the Church of Scotland.

A few days later, Mr Mack, despite his seeming physical and mental frailty, insisted on taking the funeral service of an old friend, an inhabitant of Monimaskit, conducting the event in a way which some considered not just unorthodox and irreverent, but
25 incompatible with the role of a Church of Scotland minister. After the interment he publicly repeated his story that he had met and conversed with the Devil. Finally, at the gathering in the church hall which followed, he made declarations of such a scandalous nature that the Monimaskit Kirk Session had no option but to refer the matter to the local Presbytery.

30 The procedures of the Presbyterian court system are complex, but need not long detain us. Presbytery, having heard the evidence, invited Mr Mack to defend himself. He admitted the truth of the allegations made against him, but denied that he had committed any offence. Presbytery decided to suspend him forthwith pending further investigation and consultation with the Church's legal advisers, until such time as Mr Mack
35 could be brought before a committee of Presbytery for trial. A libel was drawn up and served on him, but no date had been set for the case to be heard when Mr Mack's disappearance brought all proceedings to a halt.

MARKS

Questions

19. Using your own words as far as possible, summarise the main events that followed Gideon Mack's accident, as described in this extract. You should make **four** key points in your answer.

    4

20. Look at lines 1—11.

    By referring to **two** examples, explain how the writer uses language to suggest that Gideon's story may be untrue.

    4

21. Look at lines 12—29.

    Explain how **two** examples of language are used to describe Gideon's character after the accident.

    4

22. With reference to this extract and to elsewhere in the novel, show how an important theme is developed.

    8

[Turn over

OR

Text 3 — Prose

If you choose this text you may not attempt a question on Prose in Section 2.

Read the extract below and then attempt the following questions.

Kidnapped **by Robert Louis Stevenson**

In this extract David Balfour has arrived at the house of Shaws where his uncle Ebenezer lives. Ebenezer has asked David to fetch a chest of family papers from the stair-tower.

It was so dark inside, it seemed a body could scarce breathe; but I pushed out with foot and hand, and presently struck the wall with the one, and the lowermost round of the stair with the other. The wall, by the touch, was of fine hewn stone; the steps too, though somewhat steep and narrow, were of polished mason-work, and regular and solid under
5   foot. Minding my uncle's word about the banisters, I kept close to the tower side, and felt my way in the pitch darkness with a beating heart.

The house of Shaws stood some five full storeys high, not counting lofts. Well, as I advanced, it seemed to me the stair grew airier and a thought more lightsome; and I was wondering what might be the cause of this change, when a second blink of the summer lightning came and
10   went. If I did not cry out, it was because fear had me by the throat; and if I did not fall, it was more by Heaven's mercy than my own strength. It was not only that the flash shone in on every side through breaches in the wall, so that I seemed to be clambering aloft upon an open scaffold, but the same passing brightness showed me the steps were of unequal length, and that one of my feet rested that moment within two inches of the well.

15   This was the grand stair! I thought; and with the thought, a gust of a kind of angry courage came into my heart. My uncle had sent me here, certainly to run great risks, perhaps to die. I swore I would settle that 'perhaps', if I should break my neck for it; got me down upon my hands and knees; and as slowly as a snail, feeling before me every inch, and testing the solidity of every stone, I continued to ascend the stair. The darkness, by
20   contrast with the flash, appeared to have redoubled; nor was that all, for my ears were now troubled and my mind confounded by a great stir of bats in the top part of the tower, and the foul beasts, flying downwards, sometimes beat about my face and body.

The tower, I should have said, was square; and in every corner the step was made of a great stone of a different shape, to join the flights. Well, I had come close to one of these
25   turns, when, feeling forward as usual, my hand slipped upon an edge and found nothing but emptiness beyond it. The stair had been carried no higher: to set a stranger mounting it in the darkness was to send him straight to his death; and (although, thanks to the lightning and my own precautions, I was safe enough) the mere thought of the peril in which I might have stood, and the dreadful height I might have fallen from, brought out
30   the sweat upon my body and relaxed my joints.

But I knew what I wanted now, and turned and groped my way down again, with a wonderful anger in my heart. About half-way down, the wind sprang up in a clap and shook the tower, and died again; the rain followed; and before I had reached the ground level it fell in buckets. I put out my head into the storm, and looked along towards the kitchen. The door, which I had shut
35   behind me when I left, now stood open, and shed a little glimmer of light; and I thought I could see a figure standing in the rain, quite still, like a man hearkening. And then there came a blinding flash, which showed me my uncle plainly, just where I had fancied him to stand; and hard upon the heels of it, a great tow-row of thunder.

MARKS

Questions

23. Look at lines 1—6.

    By referring to **two** examples from these lines, explain how the writer creates a sense of fear and/or uncertainty. **4**

24. Look at lines 15—16.

    Using your own words as far as possible, explain what David suddenly realises at this point in the extract and how this affects his mood. **2**

25. Look at lines 23—38.

    Using your own words as far as possible, summarise the remainder of David's journey.

    You should make **four** key points. **4**

26. Look at lines 31—38.

    Explain how any **one** example of the writer's use of language in these lines contributes to the vivid description of the storm. **2**

27. With reference to this extract and to elsewhere in the novel, show how the writer uses drama and/or tension to create a powerful adventure story. **8**

[Turn over

OR

Text 4 — Prose

If you choose this text you may not attempt a question on Prose in Section 2.

Read the extract below and then attempt the following questions.

The Painter **by Iain Crichton Smith**

The narrator is describing a fight in the village.

But that was not what I meant to tell since the fight in itself, though unpleasant, was not evil. No, as I stood in the ring with the others, excited and horrified, I saw on the edge of the ring young William with his paint-brush and canvas and easel painting the fight. He was sitting comfortably on a chair which he had taken with him and there was no
5   expression on his face at all but a cold clear intensity which bothered me. It seemed in a strange way as if we were asleep. As the scythes swung to and fro, as the faces of the antagonists became more and more contorted in the fury of battle, as their cheeks were suffused with blood and rage, and their teeth were drawn back in a snarl, he sat there painting the battle, nor at any time did he make any attempt to pull his chair back from
10   the arena where they were engaged.

I cannot explain to you the feelings that seethed through me as I watched him. One feeling was partly admiration that he should be able to concentrate with such intensity that he didn't seem able to notice the danger he was in. The other feeling was one of the most bitter disgust as if I were watching a gaze that had gone beyond the human and which was as
15   indifferent to the outcome as a hawk's might be. You may think I was wrong in what I did next. I deliberately came up behind him and upset the chair so that he fell down head over heels in the middle of a brush-stroke. He turned on me such a gaze of blind fury that I was reminded of a rat which had once leapt at me from a river bank, and he would have struck me but that I pinioned his arms behind his back. I would have beaten him if his mother hadn't
20   come and taken him away, still snarling and weeping tears of rage. In spite of my almost religious fear at that moment, I tore the painting into small pieces and scattered them about the earth. Some people have since said that what I wanted to do was to protect the good name of the village but I must in all honesty say that that was not in my mind when I pushed the chair over. All that was in my mind was fury and disgust that this painter should have
25   watched this fight with such cold concentration that he seemed to think that the fight had been set up for him to paint, much as a house exists or an old wall.

It is true that after this no one would speak to our wonderful painter; we felt in him a presence more disturbing than Red Roderick who did after all recover. So disturbed were we by the incident that we would not even retain the happy paintings he had once
30   painted and which we had bought from him, those of the snow and the harvest, but tore them up and threw them on the dung heap.

MARKS

Questions

28. Look at lines 2—5 ("No, as I stood . . . bothered me").

   By referring to **one** example of the writer's use of language explain how William's reaction to the fight is made clear.

   2

29. Look at lines 6—8 ("As the scythes . . . snarl").

   With reference to **two** examples from these lines explain how the writer uses language to describe the dramatic nature of the fight.

   4

30. Look at lines 11—20 ("I cannot . . . tears of rage").

   Explain, in your own words as far as possible, why the narrator felt "admiration" and/or "bitter disgust" towards William the painter. You should make **four** key points in your answer.

   4

31. Look at lines 27—31.

   Explain, using your own words as far as possible, how the villagers react to William after the fight. You should make **two** key points in your answer.

   2

32. With reference to this extract, and to at least one other story by Iain Crichton Smith, show how the writer creates characters who do not appear to fit in with their surroundings.

   8

[Turn over

OR

Text 5 — Prose

If you choose this text you may not attempt a question on Prose in Section 2.

Read the extract below and then attempt the following questions.

***Dear Santa* by Anne Donovan**

Christmas Eve ah'm sittin on the bed in ma pyjamas wi a pad of blue lined paper and a Biro. The room is daurk but the wee bedside lamp makes a white circle that lights up the page ah'm starin at. It's hard tae find the words.

Dear Santa,

5   *Please could you*

I would like

If its no too much bother

But what is it ah'm tryin tae say? Could you make ma mammy love me? That's no Santa's job, he's there tae gie oot sweeties and toys tae weans wanst a year, so there's nae point 10 in askin him. If there is a Santa. Ah look oot the windae; the sky's dirty grey and ah don't think we'll huv a white Christmas somehow.

The door opens and ma mammy comes in. The hall light's on and her fair hair sticks oot all roon her heid, fuzzy and soft. A cannae see her face.

Are ye no asleep yet? It's nine o'clock.

15 *Ah'm writin ma letter tae Santa.*

Santa doesnae come if yer no sleepin. Look, there's Katie, sound.

She bends ower Katie's bed, where she's lyin wi wan airm stickin oot fae under the covers. Ma mammy lifts the bedclothes ower her, then turns tae me.

Hurry up and finish that letter, Alison. Ah'll pit it in fronty the fire and Santa'll get it 20 *when he comes.*

Ma mammy sits on the bed beside me while ah take a clean bit of paper and write dead slow so it's ma best writin.

Dear Santa,

Please could i have a Barbie doll, and a toy dog. I am a good girl.

25 *Love*

Alison

Ah fold the paper twice, print SANTA on the front, then gie it tae ma mammy. She pits it in her pocket and lifts the covers fur me tae get inside. Ah coorie doon, watchin her hair glowin like a halo against the blackness of the room. Ah love strokin her hair, it's that soft 30 and fuzzy but she cannae be bothered wi that and jerks her heid away, sayin don't, you'll mess it up, just lik she does when ma daddy tries tae touch it. But it's that quiet and still and she's in a good mood so ah lift ma haun and touch her hair, just a wee bit.

MARKS

Mammy, how come you've got fair hair and Katie's got fair hair and mines is broon?

You take efter yer daddy and Katie takes efter me.

35 *Ah wisht ah had fair hair.*

How? There's nothing wrang wi broon hair.

Ah wisht ah had hair lik yours.

Ma mammy smiles and the lines roon her eyes get deeper but she looks at me mair soft like.

40 *Go tae sleep hen, or Santa'll no come.*

She bends ower and kisses me, a dry kiss, barely grazin ma cheek, and before ah have time tae kiss her back she's switched off the bedside light, stood up and moved tae the door.

Night, Alison.

Night, Mammy.

45 She goes oot, nearly closin the door, but leavin a wee crack of light fallin across the bedclothes.

Questions

33. Using your own words as far as possible, summarise what happens in the extract. You should make **four** key points.   4

34. With reference to lines 1–11, explain how **two** examples of Donovan's use of language help the reader to understand how Alison finds the task of writing the letter.   4

35. Look at lines 27–46.

   (a) Explain how **one** example of Donovan's language helps the reader understand there is a **positive** aspect to Alison's relationship with her mother.   2

   (b) Explain how **one** example of Donovan's language helps the reader understand there is a **negative** aspect to Alison's relationship with her mother.   2

36. Characters in Donovan's stories often face personal difficulties. With reference to the extract and to at least one other story, show how personal difficulties are explored.   8

[Turn over

SECTION 1 — SCOTTISH TEXT — 20 marks

PART C — SCOTTISH TEXT — POETRY

Text 1 — Poetry

If you choose this text you may not attempt a question on Poetry in Section 2.

Read the poem below and then attempt the following questions.

***Originally* by Carol Ann Duffy**

We came from our own country in a red room
which fell through the fields, our mother singing
our father's name to the turn of the wheels.
My brothers cried, one of them bawling, *Home*,
5   *Home*, as the miles rushed back to the city,
the street, the house, the vacant rooms
where we didn't live any more. I stared
at the eyes of a blind toy, holding its paw.

All childhood is an emigration. Some are slow,
10   leaving you standing, resigned, up an avenue
where no one you know stays. Others are sudden.
Your accent wrong. Corners, which seem familiar,
leading to unimagined pebble-dashed estates, big boys
eating worms and shouting words you don't understand.
15   My parents' anxieties stirred like a loose tooth
in my head. *I want our own country*, I said.

But then you forget, or don't recall, or change,
and, seeing your brother swallow a slug, feel only
a skelf of shame. I remember my tongue
20   shedding its skin like a snake, my voice
in the classroom sounding just like the rest. Do I only think
I lost a river, culture, speech, sense of first space
and the right place? Now, *Where do you come from*?
strangers ask. *Originally*? And I hesitate.

Page eighteen

MARKS

Questions

37. Look at lines 1—8.

Explain, using your own words as far as possible, what the poet/persona remembers about the journey. You should make **two** key points.   2

38. By referring to **two** examples of the poet's use of language in lines 9—16, explain fully how the poet makes clear the effect(s) of moving home.   4

39. Look at lines 17—21 ("But then . . . like the rest").

By referring to **two** examples of the poet's use of language explain fully how the poet suggests acceptance of the move.   4

40. Look at the last four words of the poem ("*Originally*? . . . hesitate").

Explain how any part of this makes an effective ending to the poem.   2

41. By referring closely to this poem, and to at least one other poem by Duffy, show how the poet uses word choice and/or imagery effectively to convey theme(s).   8

[Turn over

OR

Text 2 — Poetry

If you choose this text you may not attempt a question on Poetry in Section 2.

Read the poem below and then attempt the following questions.

***Good Friday* by Edwin Morgan**

Three o'clock. The bus lurches
round into the sun. 'D's this go – '
he flops beside me – 'right along Bath Street?
– Oh tha's, tha's all right, see I've
5   got to get some Easter eggs for the kiddies.
I've had a wee drink, ye understand –
ye'll maybe think it's a – funny day
to be celebrating – well, no, but ye see
I wasny working, and I like to celebrate
10   when I'm no working – I don't say it's right
I'm no saying it's right, ye understand – ye understand?
But anyway tha's the way I look at it –
I'm no boring you, eh? – ye see today,
take today, I don't know what today's in aid of,
15   whether Christ was – crucified or was he –
rose fae the dead like, see what I mean?
You're an educatit man, you can tell me –
– Aye, well. There ye are. It's been seen
time and again, the working man
20   has nae education, he jist canny – jist
hasny got it, know what I mean,
he's jist bliddy ignorant – Christ aye,
bliddy ignorant. Well –' The bus brakes violently,
he lunges for the stair, swings down – off,
25   into the sun for his Easter eggs,
on very
        nearly
            steady
                legs.

MARKS

Questions

42. Look at lines 2—13 ("D's this go . . . boring you, eh?").

    By referring to two examples of his speech, explain **two** things we learn about the drunk man.

    4

43. Look at lines 14—23.

    (a) Comment on the effectiveness of **one** feature of the poet's use of language in creating realistic speech.

    2

    (b) Show how any **two** examples of the use of word choice makes clear the poem's main ideas or central concerns.

    4

44. How effective do you find lines 23—29 as a conclusion to the poem? You should refer to **one** example from these lines and to the ideas and/or language of the rest of the poem.

    2

45. By referring closely to this poem and to at least one other poem, show how Morgan explores important human themes.

    8

[Turn over

OR

Text 3 — Poetry

If you choose this text you may not attempt a question on Poetry in Section 2.

Read the poem below and then attempt the following questions.

Sounds of the day **by Norman MacCaig**

When a clatter came,
it was horses crossing the ford.
When the air creaked, it was
a lapwing seeing us off the premises
5   of its private marsh. A snuffling puff
ten yards from the boat was the tide blocking and
unblocking a hole in a rock.
When the black drums rolled, it was water
falling sixty feet into itself.

10   When the door
scraped shut, it was the end
of all the sounds there are.

You left me
beside the quietest fire in the world.

15   I thought I was hurt in my pride only,
forgetting that,
when you plunge your hand in freezing water,
you feel
a bangle of ice round your wrist
20   before the whole hand goes numb.

MARKS

Questions

46. Look at lines 1—9.

Explain fully, in your own words as far as possible, how the poet feels about the "sounds of the day".

2

47. Look again at lines 1—9.

By referring to **one** example of the poet's word choice, explain how the poet suggests that disturbance or upset is to follow.

2

48. Look at lines 10—14.

By referring to **two** examples of the writer's use of language, explain fully how the poet makes it clear that the mood or atmosphere of the poem has now changed.

4

49. Look at lines 15—20.

By referring to **two** examples of word choice or imagery, explain fully how the poet makes clear the effects of his experience.

4

50. By referring to this poem, and to at least one other by MacCaig, show how strong feelings are a feature of his poetry.

8

[Turn over

OR

Text 4 — Poetry

If you choose this text you may not attempt a question on Poetry in Section 2.

Read the poem below and then attempt the following questions.

Keeping Orchids **by Jackie Kay**

The orchids my mother gave me when we first met
are still alive, twelve days later. Although

some of the buds remain closed as secrets.
Twice since I carried them back, like a baby in a shawl,

5   from her train station to mine, then home. Twice
since then the whole glass carafe has crashed

falling over, unprovoked, soaking my chest of drawers.
All the broken waters. I have rearranged

the upset orchids with troubled hands. Even after
10   that the closed ones did not open out. The skin

shut like an eye in the dark; the closed lid.
Twelve days later, my mother's hands are all I have.

Her face is fading fast. Even her voice rushes
through a tunnel the other way from home.

15   I close my eyes and try to remember exactly:
a paisley pattern scarf, a brooch, a navy coat.

A digital watch her daughter was wearing when she died.
Now they hang their heads,

and suddenly grow old — the proof of meeting. Still,
20   her hands, awkward and hard to hold

fold and unfold a green carrier bag as she tells
the story of her life. Compressed. Airtight.

A sad square, then a crumpled shape. A bag of tricks.
Her secret life — a hidden album, a box of love letters.

25   A door opens and closes. Time is outside waiting.
I catch the draught in my winter room.

Airlocks keep the cold air out.
Boiling water makes flowers live longer. So does

cutting the stems with a sharp knife.

MARKS

Questions

51. Using your own words as far as possible, explain what happens in lines 1—10 of this poem. You should make **two** key points.   2

52. Look again at lines 1—13 ("The orchids . . . fading fast.").

    Explain how the poet uses **one** example of word choice and **one** feature of structure to develop the idea of time.   4

53. Look at lines 13—29 ("Even her voice . . . sharp knife.").

    By referring to **three** examples of the poet's use of language, explain how the poet creates a sense of awkwardness about the meeting.   6

54. By referring closely to this poem and to at least one other poem by Kay, show how the poet uses personal experience to explore wider themes.   8

[END OF SECTION 1]

[Turn over

SECTION 2 — CRITICAL ESSAY — 20 marks

Attempt ONE question from the following genres — Drama, Prose, Poetry, Film and Television Drama, or Language.

Your answer must be on a different genre from that chosen in Section 1.

You should spend approximately 45 minutes on this Section.

DRAMA

Answers to questions in this part should refer to the text and to such relevant features as characterisation, key scene(s), structure, climax, theme, plot, conflict, setting . . .

1. Choose a play which explores an important relationship, for example, husband and wife, leader and follower, parent and child, or any other relationship.

   Describe this relationship and then, by referring to appropriate techniques, explain how the relationship develops.

2. Choose a play which explores an issue or theme which interests you.

   By referring to appropriate techniques, explain how this issue or theme is explored.

PROSE

Answers to questions in this part should refer to the text and to such relevant features as characterisation, setting, language, key incident(s), climax, turning point, plot, structure, narrative technique, theme, ideas, description . . .

3. Choose a novel **or** short story **or** work of non-fiction which has a key moment.

   Give a brief account of the key moment and, by referring to appropriate techniques, show how it is significant to the text as a whole.

4. Choose a novel **or** short story in which there is an interesting character.

   By referring to appropriate techniques, show how the author makes the character interesting.

POETRY

> *Answers to questions in this part should refer to the text and to such relevant features as word choice, tone, imagery, structure, content, rhythm, rhyme, theme, sound, ideas . . .*

5. Choose a poem which describes a person or a place or an event in a memorable way.

    By referring to poetic techniques, explain how the poet makes this poem so memorable.

6. Choose a poem which deals with a powerful emotion.

    By referring to poetic techniques, show how the poet creates the powerful emotion.

FILM AND TELEVISION DRAMA

> *Answers to questions in this part should refer to the text and to such relevant features as use of camera, key sequence, characterisation, mise-en-scène, editing, setting, music/sound, special effects, plot, dialogue . . .*

7. Choose a scene or sequence from a film or TV drama which shocks or surprises you in some way.

    By referring to appropriate techniques, show how in this scene or sequence the element of surprise is made effective.

8. Choose a film or TV drama in which there is a character about whom you have mixed feelings.

    Show why this character is important to the film or TV drama as a whole and by referring to appropriate techniques, explain how these mixed feelings are created.

* "TV drama" includes a single play, a series or a serial.

[Turn over

LANGUAGE

> *Answers to questions in this part should refer to the text and to such relevant features as register, accent, dialect, slang, jargon, vocabulary, tone, abbreviation . . .*

9. Choose an advertisement which aims to persuade you to buy a product, or to support the aims of a particular group.

   By referring to specific examples from the advertisement, explain how persuasive language is used.

10. Consider the distinctive language used by any group of people from the same place, or with the same job, or the same interest . . .

   By referring to specific examples, explain how the distinctive language of the group is different from the language used by the general population.

[END OF SECTION 2]

[END OF QUESTION PAPER]

NATIONAL 5

2017

National Qualifications 2017

X724/75/11

English
Reading for Understanding, Analysis and Evaluation

FRIDAY, 12 MAY

9:00 AM – 10:00 AM

Total marks — 30

Attempt ALL questions.

Write your answers clearly in the answer booklet provided. In the answer booklet you must clearly identify the question number you are attempting.

Use **blue** or **black** ink.

Before leaving the examination room you must give your answer booklet to the Invigilator; if you do not, you may lose all the marks for this paper.

Resilience

My best friend, Mark, was a keen footballer. We played in my back garden every afternoon as kids, often down the local park, sometimes other kids would join us, and in the summer we never seemed to leave.

I often think of those long, endlessly absorbing days, game after game, sometimes until it got dark
5 and we played by the dim glow of street lights. In the summer holidays, my mum would make a two-litre bottle of orange squash and we would pass it from player to player at half-time, none of us deterred by the fact it had got warm in the sun. My, it tasted good.

Mark never made it into the school team. He kept trying, kept going to the "trials", both at primary and senior school, but he was just off the pace. The disappointment was always bitter.
10 You could see it on his face. He yearned to play, to progress, to be able to read out a match report at school assembly (one of the honours of making the team). But he never did.

It has been reported that 98 per cent of those signed by English teams at 16 fail to make the transition into professional football. Many struggle to cope with rejection at such a tender age. Clinical psychologists report that many suffer anxiety, a loss of confidence and, in some cases,
15 depression. These youngsters are often described as being "left on football's scrapheap".

It seems to me, though, that the number rejected is, in fact, far higher. After all, the sifting process starts from the first time you kick a ball at the local park. I was one of the few who made it into my school team (I captained it). But when I went to trial for the district team, surrounded by the best players from all the schools in the area, the standard was high. Parents were
20 everywhere. I remember my heart beating out of my chest when the "scouts" arrived. I did not make it. I was crushed by the disappointment. How could it be otherwise? But I also realised that the race had only just started for those who had made the cut. Of those who made it into the district team, only a handful were picked by Reading, the local club. And of those who made it to Reading, only a fraction made it into professional football. Perhaps none made it all the way to
25 the top flight.

And that really is the point. When we watch any Premier League match, we are witnessing players who have made it through a filtering process of staggering dimensions. It is a process that does not merely discard 98 per cent of those who aspire, but something closer to 99·9999 per cent. For every first-team player, there are millions of others, like grains of sand on the beach, who have
30 tried, who have dreamt, but who have failed.

The majority, like Mark, never made it through the first lap. Others made it to the final straight, before dropping out. But this is football. This is life. Failure is an inevitable aspect of any competition worthy of the name. Without losers, there cannot be winners. Without pain, there cannot be joy. Without natural selection, there cannot be evolution. Failure is not the opposite of
35 progress; failure is part and parcel of progress.

Take a step back and you will see that football is a beautiful meritocracy. That so many dreams are shattered is testament to just how many dared to dream in the first place. The skills are transparent, the opportunities exist. There is no room for family favours or cosy alliances. The best of the best shine through, whether they are from a tough part of Liverpool, like Wayne
40 Rooney, or raised in grinding poverty in Uruguay, like Luis Suárez.

And the important point is that clubs have a responsibility to those who make it as far as the academies. They have a responsibility to create rounded people, with decent educations. Parents must support this approach, too, rather than exerting undue pressure on often vulnerable children. This is not just about giving youngsters a plan B; it is also about enlightened
45 self-interest.

Youngsters who are educated and self-assured are likely to be better footballers, too. The Ancient Greeks understood this only too well. They created strong links between the gymnasiums and the academies and embraced the humane idea that the mind and body grow together. The German football system has embraced this truth, too. The clubs there want intelligent and confident
50 young men. Such a cultural transformation needs to happen here, too. But I wish to make a deeper point. It is that we need to redefine our relationship with failure, not just in football but in life. We need to remind our children that losing is an essential (indeed, a beautiful) part of life. We need to emphasise the empowering idea that failure is less important, infinitely less so, than how we respond to it. Failing to make the grade at football is crushing. It is natural to be sad. But
55 it is also a pathway to a new reality.

Tens of thousands do not make it to Oxford or Cambridge. Hundreds of thousands of actors never win an Oscar. Tens of millions fail to make it into Manchester United or Chelsea. But this is not the end of life. It is merely the beginning. It is an opportunity to conceive a new dream, a new hope, a new way of finding meaning in this curious journey called life.

60 I often think about Mark. And I am thankful that his failures in football, so important, so trivial, never deterred him. He created new dreams, new aspirations, and lived a life that inspired all who knew him.

Life is too short, too precious, to be derailed by failure. We have to accept it. We have to embrace it.

Matthew Syed, in "The Times"

MARKS

Total marks — 30

Attempt ALL Questions

1. Look at lines 1—7, and explain how **one** example of the writer's word choice makes it clear that his memories of childhood football are positive.

   2

2. Look at lines 8—11, and explain **in your own words** why Mark was so disappointed.

   You should make **four** key points in your answer.

   4

3. Look at lines 12—25, and identify **in your own words six** points which the writer makes about young people hoping to become professional footballers.

   6

4. Explain fully why the simile "like grains of sand on the beach" (line 29) is effective here.

   2

5. Look at lines 31—35. By referring to **two** language features, explain how the writer makes clear his view about competition.

   You should refer to **two different** features such as word choice, imagery or sentence structure.

   4

6. The writer tells us that "football is a beautiful meritocracy" (line 36).

   Explain **in your own words three** points the writer makes about merit being rewarded in the rest of this paragraph.

   3

7. Look at lines 46—55, and identify, **in your own words** as far as possible, **five** points the writer makes in these lines about sport and/or life.

   5

8. Look at lines 56—59, and explain how **one** feature of the writer's sentence structure is used to highlight an important point.

   2

9. Select any expression in lines 60—64, and explain how it contributes to the passage's effective conclusion.

   2

[END OF QUESTION PAPER]

National
Qualifications
2017

X724/75/12

English
Critical Reading

FRIDAY, 12 MAY

10:20 AM – 11:50 AM

Total marks — 40

SECTION 1 — Scottish Text — 20 marks

Read an extract from a Scottish text you have previously studied.

Choose ONE text from either

Part A — Drama   Pages 2–7

or

Part B — Prose   Pages 8–17

or

Part C — Poetry   Pages 18–25

Attempt ALL the questions for your chosen text.

SECTION 2 — Critical Essay — 20 marks

Attempt ONE question from the following genres — Drama, Prose, Poetry, Film and Television Drama, or Language.

Your answer must be on a different genre from that chosen in Section 1.

You should spend approximately 45 minutes on each Section.

Write your answers clearly in the answer booklet provided. In the answer booklet you must clearly identify the question number you are attempting.

Use **blue** or **black** ink.

Before leaving the examination room you must give your answer booklet to the Invigilator; if you do not, you may lose all the marks for this paper.

SECTION 1 — SCOTTISH TEXT — 20 marks

PART A — SCOTTISH TEXT — DRAMA

Text 1 — Drama

If you choose this text you may not attempt a question on Drama in Section 2.

Read the extract below and then attempt the following questions.

***Bold Girls* by Rona Munro**

Extract from Scene Two (The women are in a social club . . .)

	CASSIE:	It's the D.T.s.
	NORA:	It's the R.U.C.
	CASSIE:	Oh don't let it get to you.
	NORA:	So let's see your hand!
5		*Cassie holds hers out, it is also shaking*
	CASSIE:	It's our life style Mummy, we'll have to change our life style.
	NORA:	Is that right?
	CASSIE:	We're living too fast so we are, it's the same problem the film stars have, we'll burn ourselves out with all the excitement.
10	NORA:	Me and Joan Collins both.
	CASSIE:	You can write articles for the women's magazines, "Stop and Search, would your manicure stand up to the closest inspection?"
	NORA:	Let's see Marie's hand there.
		Marie is lost in her own thoughts
15		*Cassie pulls Marie's hand out, Nora and Cassie study it*
	CASSIE:	Steady as a rock.
	NORA:	Ah she's got a clear conscience.
	CASSIE:	Either that or she's in a coma, are you with us, Marie?
	MARIE:	Hmmm?
20	NORA:	Wired up but not plugged in.
	MARIE:	Are you reading my palm?
	CASSIE:	I will if you like.
		Deirdre approaches their table with a tray of drinks
		Cassie glances up at her, then bends theatrically over Marie's hand
25	CASSIE:	Oh, you're going to meet a dark stranger Marie, all in white but with a black wee heart. You better watch out for she'll thieve the clothes off your back but you'll not have peace till you nail the wee snake down and ask her what she's up to.

MARKS

30	DEIRDRE:	(*handing out the drinks correctly*) Black Russian — gin and lime — Pernod and blackcurrant.
	CASSIE:	So what about you Deirdre, if it is Deirdre?
	DEIRDRE:	It is.
	MARIE:	Cassie . . .
35	CASSIE:	I hope you've not taken a fancy to anything else that's caught your eye, like my handbag.
	DEIRDRE:	(*staring at Cassie for a minute*) It was in a car. A blue car.
	CASSIE:	What?
	DEIRDRE:	That I saw you before.
	CASSIE:	You're a lying hoor, you never saw anything.
40	DEIRDRE:	With a man. With him. With —
		Cassie lunges at her before she can get another word out

Questions

1. Using your own words as far as possible, identify **four** things you learn about the women's lives in this extract.   4

2. Look at lines 1—12.

    Identify **one** example of humour and explain why it is effective.   2

3. Look at lines 13—35.

    (a) By referring to **one** example of word choice, explain how the playwright reveals the relationship between Nora and Marie.   2

    (b) By referring to **one** example of word choice, explain how the playwright reveals the relationship between Cassie and Deirdre.   2

4. Look at lines 36—41.

    By referring to **one** example of the writer's use of language, explain how this extract ends with a moment of tension.   2

5. By referring to this extract and to elsewhere in the play, show how mother and daughter-type relationships are explored.   8

[Turn over

OR

Text 2 — Drama

If you choose this text you may not attempt a question on Drama in Section 2.

Read the extract below and then attempt the following questions.

Sailmaker **by Alan Spence**

ALEC: What is it that gets intae ye? Wi the bettin ah mean?

DAVIE: Ah don't know. Just wan a these things.

　　　　　Ah suppose it's the feelin you've at least got a *chance*.

　　　　　Is there any wood in there? The paper just flares up then dies.

5　　　　(*ALEC empties out contents of box, hands box to DAVIE*)

DAVIE: Great. (*Starts breaking up box, ALEC goes out, comes back with canvas tool-bag, cane bow. Fires imaginary arrow*) Bring me my bow of burning gold, eh?

　　　　　(*ALEC breaks bow for fire*)

　　　　　That's more like it. (*Warms himself*)

10　　　　That's the stuff.

ALEC: (*Taking tools from canvas bag*) Look at this.

DAVIE: God. Ma auld sailmakin tools. (*Takes wooden marlinspike*) Ah was an apprentice when ah was your age. Hard work it wis tae.

　　　　　Ah worked on the Queen Mary ye know.

15　ALEC: Aye.

DAVIE: Worked on destroyers durin the War. Made gun-covers, awnings, tarpaulins.

　　　　　Made this wee bag!

ALEC: Did ye?

DAVIE: Oh aye. Used tae make leather wallets an things.

20　　　　Made a shopping bag for yer mother. Made you a swing! Wi a big sorta bucket seat. Used tae hang it in the doorway there.

ALEC: Ah remember!

　　　　　You could still be makin things. Sellin them.

　　　　　(*DAVIE nods, shrugs*)

25　　　　Could ye no go back tae yer trade?

DAVIE: Nae demand. Was different durin the War. They needed us then awright. Reserved occupation it was. Meant ah couldnae sign up. Been goin downhill since then but. Yards shuttin doon. Look at Harland's. Or where it was. Just a big empty space covered wi weeds.

30　　　　Yer Uncle Billy had the right idea. Took his redundancy money and moved tae Aberdeen. Doin all right.

ALEC: Ian's an Aberdeen supporter now.

MARKS

DAVIE: Billy'll disown him for that!

ALEC: Did you ever think about movin?

35 DAVIE: Thought about it. (*Shrugs*) Thing is Billy bein a painter had more chance ae a job. Ah backed a loser right fae the start. Then it got even worse. They started bringin in aw the manmade fibres, usin machines. Got lassies daein hauf the work. Dead loss.

So for God's sake you dae somethin wi *your* life!

Questions

6. By referring to **two** examples from anywhere in this extract, explain how Alec's attitude towards Davie is revealed at this point in the play.   4

7. Look at lines 14—21.

By referring to **two** examples of language, explain how the writer suggests Davie's enthusiasm for his old trade.   4

8. Look at lines 26—38.

By referring to **two** examples of language, explain how the writer makes it clear that Davie's old trade is not important any more.   4

9. By referring to this extract and to elsewhere in the play, show how the character of Davie is presented.   8

[Turn over

OR

Text 3 — Drama

If you choose this text you may not attempt a question on Drama in Section 2.

Read the extract below and then attempt the following questions.

Tally's Blood by Ann Marie Di Mambro

	ROSINELLA:	You don't see it, do you? It's up to me to see everything.
	MASSIMO:	See what?
	ROSINELLA:	Why do you think she was in that state, eh?
	MASSIMO:	Over the wedding.
5	ROSINELLA:	Stupid eejit. Over Hughie, you mean.
	MASSIMO:	Hughie?
	ROSINELLA:	You no see the way he looks at our Lucia? He's crazy for her.
	MASSIMO:	Away you go. They grew up together.
	ROSINELLA:	She's to marry an Italian.
10	MASSIMO:	For God's sake, Rosie, she's no asking to marry him, just to go to his brother's wedding. You worry too much.
	ROSINELLA:	No, Massimo. I don't worry enough. It's been going on before my eyes and I've never seen it till tonight.
	MASSIMO:	Seen what?
15	ROSINELLA:	It's bad enough he's fell for her. But don't tell me she's to get falling for him. I'll soon put a stop to this before it starts.
	MASSIMO:	(*Groans*) Rosie . . .
	ROSINELLA:	Italians are not interested in a lassie that's been out with anybody else — especially the Scotch men. They like a girl that's kept herself for them. I'm surprised at you.
20		
	MASSIMO:	What have I done now?
	ROSINELLA:	Are you forgetting what this country did to the Italians during the war? (*Massimo groans*) They took you out of here as if you were a thief.
25	MASSIMO:	Listen, Rosie, all I care about the war is that it's over. I lost ma faither, ma brother and four years out ma life.
	ROSINELLA:	Well, I'll never get over it.
	MASSIMO:	Neither will I. But everybody suffered. Not just us.
	ROSINELLA:	Italians have got to stick together.
	MASSIMO:	Then come to Italy with me, Rosie, what do you say?
30		*Rosinella uncomfortable at mention of Italy.*
	ROSINELLA:	No . . . I don't think so.
	MASSIMO:	A wee holiday. The three of us.

MARKS

ROSINELLA: Not yet, Massimo. You go, yourself. I don't mind.

35

MASSIMO: Everybody was asking for you when I was over. Asking why you've never been back. Please, Rosie, I'm dying to show you my daddy's house. You can help me make it nice. Next year, maybe, eh? How about it, Rosie?

ROSINELLA: I'm not going anywhere, Massimo, not until I see Lucia settled. (*A beat*) You think she's calmed down now? I think I'll take her to Glasgow on Saturday, go round the shops, get her something nice, take her to Palombo's to get her hair done. I'll go and tell her.

40

Questions

10. Look at lines 1—17.

Using your own words as far as possible, identify the key areas of disagreement between Rosinella and Massimo. You should make **four** key points in your answer.   4

11. Look at lines 9—20.

By referring to **two** examples of language, explain what is revealed about Rosinella's character.   4

12. Look at lines 22—27.

By referring to **two** examples from their dialogue, explain how Rosinella and Massimo's different attitudes to the war are revealed.   4

13. By referring to this extract and to elsewhere in the play, show how the character of Massimo is presented.   8

[Turn over

SECTION 1 — SCOTTISH TEXT — 20 marks

PART B — SCOTTISH TEXT — PROSE

Text 1 — Prose

If you choose this text you may not attempt a question on Prose in Section 2.

Read the extract below and then attempt the following questions.

The Cone-Gatherers **by Robin Jenkins**

In this extract from Chapter One, Duror is watching the cone-gatherers' hut.

The hut was lit by oil-lamp. He smelled paraffin as well as woodsmoke. He knew they picked up old cones to kindle the fire, and on Sunday they had worked for hours sawing up blown timber for firewood: they had been given permission to do so. The only window was not in the wall facing him, so that he could not see inside; but he had been in their hut so
5   often, they were in his imagination so vividly, and he was so close every sound they made could be interpreted; therefore it was easy for him to picture them as they went about making their meal. They peeled their potatoes the night before, and left them in a pot of cold water. They did not wash before they started to cook or eat. They did not change their clothes. They had no table; an upturned box did instead, with a newspaper for a
10   cloth; and each sat on his own bed. They seldom spoke. All evening they would be dumb, the taller brooding over a days-old paper, the dwarf carving some animal out of wood: at present he was making a squirrel. Seeing it half-finished that afternoon, holding it shudderingly in his hands, Duror had against his will, against indeed the whole frenzied thrust of his being, sensed the kinship between the carver and the creature whose likeness
15   he was carving. When complete, the squirrel would be not only recognisable, it would be almost alive. To Duror it had been the final defeat that such ability should be in a half-man, a freak, an imbecile. He had read that the Germans were putting idiots and cripples to death in gas chambers. Outwardly, as everybody expected, he condemned such barbarity; inwardly, thinking of idiocy and crippledness not as abstractions but as
20   embodied in the crouch-backed cone-gatherer, he had profoundly approved.

At last he roused himself and moved away. Yet, though he was going home, he felt he was leaving behind him in that hut something unresolved, which would never cease to torment him. It was almost as if there were not two brothers, but three; he himself was the third. Once he halted and looked back. His fists tightened on his gun. He saw himself returning,
25   kicking open the door, shouting at them his disgust, and then blasting them both to everlasting perdition. He felt an icy hand on his brow as he imagined that hideous but liberating fratricide.

MARKS

Questions

14. Look at lines 1—12.

Using your own words as far as possible, identify **four** things we learn about how the cone-gatherers live.   **4**

15. Look at lines 12—20.

By referring to **two** examples of language, explain how the writer makes clear Duror's feelings towards the cone-gatherers.   **4**

16. Look at lines 21—27.

By referring to **two** examples of language, explain how Duror feels at this point.   **4**

17. By referring to this extract and to elsewhere in the novel, show how the theme of good versus evil is explored.   **8**

[Turn over

OR

Text 2 — Prose

If you choose this text you may not attempt a question on Prose in Section 2.

Read the extract below and then attempt the following questions.

The Testament of Gideon Mack by James Robertson

This extract is taken from the section of the novel where Gideon is relating his experience in the cave with the Devil after falling into the Black Jaws.

"You must understand," I said, "that I've never seriously thought you existed at all. It's a bit of a shock now, to find you just a few miles from Monimaskit."

"Don't think you're privileged," he said, sparking up a bit. "Don't think I'm paying you some kind of special attention. I do like Scotland, though, I spend a lot of time here. I once
5   preached to some women at North Berwick who thought they were witches. They were burnt for it, poor cows. I preached at Auchtermuchty another time, disguised as one of your lot, a minister, but the folk there found me out. Fifers, thrawn buggers, they were too sharp. But I do like Scotland. I like the miserable weather. I like the miserable people, the fatalism, the negativity, the violence that's always just below the surface. And I like the way
10   you deal with religion. One century you're up to your lugs in it, the next you're trading the whole apparatus in for Sunday superstores. Praise the Lord and thrash the bairns. Ask and ye shall have the door shut in your face. Blessed are they that shop on the Sabbath, for they shall get the best bargains. Oh, yes, this is a very fine country."

In spite of his claimed affection for Scotland, he seemed morose and fed up. Suddenly he
15   brightened.

"I know what I'll do if you want proof. I'll do what I said I would. I'll fix your leg."

This did not strike me as a good idea. "No," I said. "A surgeon should do that."

"Please," he said. "I'd like to."

When I said no again I heard a low rumble growl round the cave, which I took to be the
20   precursor of another stupendous roar. I made no further protest. He went over to the fire and I saw him put his right hand into the flames, deep into the middle of them. He was elbow-deep in fire but he didn't even flinch. His jacket didn't catch alight, and his hand and arm were quite unaffected by the heat. He stayed like that for fully three minutes. Then he turned and his whole arm was a white, pulsating glow. He came towards me and
25   reached for my leg with that terrible arm, and I shrank away from him.

"It doesn't hurt me," he said, "and it won't hurt you. Don't move."

I was too terrified to move. I was still clutching my mug of tea and he took it from me with his left hand and placed it on the ground. I closed my eyes and waited for the burning agony, but it did not come. I was aware only of a slight tingling sensation on my right thigh.
30   I opened my eyes and looked down. There was intense concentration on his face. His hand was *inside* my leg. Where the bone bulged out the skin was sizzling and popping like bacon in a pan, but there was no pain, only this faint tickle. He was pushing and prodding the bone back into place, welding it together. Smoke snd steam issued from my leg, but still there was no pain. I felt only an incredible warmth, like the warmth of the spirit in his
35   black bottle, spreading through my whole body. His hand twisted something and my leg gave an involuntary jolt. "Don't move," he snapped. "I couldn't help it," I said.

MARKS

Questions

18. Look at lines 3—18.

    Using your own words as far as possible, identify **three** things we learn about the Devil.

    3

19. Look at lines 19—36.

    By referring to **one** example, explain how language is used to show Gideon's fear.

    2

20. Look again at lines 19—36.

    Using your own words as far as possible, explain how the Devil fixes Gideon's leg. You should make **three** key points in your answer.

    3

21. In this extract the devil's mood changes. By referring to **two** examples of language from anywhere in the extract, explain how the writer makes this clear.

    4

22. By referring to this extract and to elsewhere in the novel, show how meeting the Devil affects the character of Gideon Mack.

    8

[Turn over

OR

Text 3 — Prose

If you choose this text you may not attempt a question on Prose in Section 2.

Read the extract below and then attempt the following questions.

Kidnapped **by Robert Louis Stevenson**

In this extract from Chapter 20, David Balfour and Alan Breck Stewart are on the run after the killing of Red Fox.

The first peep of morning, then, showed us this horrible place, and I could see Alan knit his brow.

"This is no fit place for you and me," he said. "This is a place they're bound to watch."

And with that he ran harder than ever down to the water side, in a part where the river
5 was split in two among three rocks. It went through with a horrid thundering that made my belly quake; and there hung over the lynn a little mist of spray. Alan looked neither to the right nor to the left, but jumped clean upon the middle rock and fell there on his hands and knees to check himself, for that rock was small and he might have pitched over on the far side. I had scarce time to measure the distance or to understand the peril before I had
10 followed him, and he had caught and stopped me.

So there we stood, side by side upon a small rock slippery with spray, a far broader leap in front of us, and the river dinning upon all sides. When I saw where I was, there came on me a deadly sickness of fear, and I put my hand over my eyes. Alan took me and shook me; I saw he was speaking, but the roaring of the falls and the trouble of my mind prevented me
15 from hearing; only I saw his face was red with anger, and that he stamped upon the rock. The same look showed me the water raging by, and the mist hanging in the air: and with that I covered my eyes again and shuddered.

The next minute Alan had set the brandy bottle to my lips, and forced me to drink about a gill, which sent the blood into my head again. Then, putting his hands to his mouth and his
20 mouth to my ear, he shouted, "Hang or drown!" and turning his back upon me, leaped over the farther branch of the stream, and landed safe.

I was now alone upon the rock, which gave me the more room; the brandy was singing in my ears; I had this good example fresh before me, and just wit enough to see that if I did not leap at once, I should never leap at all. I bent low on my knees and flung myself forth,
25 with that kind of anger of despair that has sometimes stood me in stead of courage. Sure enough, it was but my hands that reached the full length; these slipped, caught again, slipped again; and I was sliddering back into the lynn, when Alan seized me, first by the hair, then by the collar, and with a great strain dragged me into safety.

Never a word he said, but set off running again for his life, and I must stagger to my feet
30 and run after him. I had been weary before, but now I was sick and bruised, and partly drunken with the brandy; I kept stumbling as I ran, I had a stitch that came near to overmaster me; and when at last Alan paused under a great rock that stood there among a number of others, it was none too soon for David Balfour.

MARKS

Questions

23. Using your own words as far as possible, summarise the main events in this extract. You should make **four** key points in your answer.   4

24. Look at lines 1—10.

    (a) Explain how **one** example of the writer's language shows that Alan is confident at this point in the extract.   2

    (b) Explain how **one** example of the writer's language shows how David feels at this point in the extract.   2

25. Look at lines 22—28.

    Explain how **one** example of sentence structure and **one** example of word choice contribute to the creation of drama at this point in the extract.   4

26. By referring to this extract and to elsewhere in the novel, show the ways in which Alan supports David physically **and/or** emotionally throughout the novel.   8

[Turn over

OR

Text 4 — Prose

If you choose this text you may not attempt a question on Prose in Section 2.

Read the extract below and then attempt the following questions.

The Crater by Iain Crichton Smith

On his hands and knees he squirmed forward, the others behind him. This was his first raid and he thought, "I am frightened." But it was different from being out in the open on a battlefield. It was an older fear, the fear of being buried in the earth, the fear of wandering through eternal passageways and meeting grey figures like weasels and fighting
5   with them in the darkness. He tested the wire. Thank God it had been cut. And then he thought, "Will we need the ladders?" The sides of the trenches were so deep sometimes that ladders were necessary to get out again. And as he crawled towards the German trenches he had a vision of Germans crawling beneath British trenches undermining them. A transparent imagined web hung below him in the darkness quivering with grey spiders.

10   He looked at his illuminated watch. The time was right. Then they were in the German trenches. The rest was a series of thrustings and flashes. Once he thought he saw or imagined he saw from outside a dugout a man sitting inside reading a book. It was like looking through a train window into a house before the house disappears. There were Mills bombs, hackings of bayonets, scurryings and breathings as of rats. A white face towered
15   above him, his pistol exploded and the face disappeared. There was a terrible stink all around him, and the flowing of blood. Then there was a long silence. Back. They must get back. He passed the order along. And then they wriggled back again avoiding the craters which lay around them, created by shells, and which were full of slimy water. If they fell into one of these they would be drowned. As he looked, shells began to fall into them
20   sending up huge spouts of water. Over the parapet. They were over the parapet. Crouched they had run and scrambled and were over. Two of them were carrying a third. They stumbled down the trench. There were more wounded than he had thought. Wright . . . one arm seemed to have been shot off. Sergeant Smith was bending over him. "You'll get sent home all right," he was saying. Some of the men were tugging at their equipment and
25   talking feverishly. Young Ellis was lying down, blood pouring from his mouth. Harris said, "Morrison's in the crater."

He and Sergeant Smith looked at each other. They were both thinking the same: there is no point, he's had it. They could see each other's eyes glaring whitely through the black, but could not tell the expression on the faces. The shells were still falling, drumming and
30   shaking the earth. All these craters out there, these dead moons.

MARKS

Questions

27. Look at lines 1—9.

    By referring to **two** examples, explain how the writer's use of language makes clear the soldier's fear.   **4**

28. Look at lines 11—16 ("The rest . . . flowing of blood").

    Using your own words as far as possible, identify **four** ways in which the trenches are horrific.   **4**

29. Look at lines 16—21 ("Back . . . and were over").

    By referring to **one** example, explain how the sentence structure highlights the danger faced by the men.   **2**

30. Look at lines 27—30.

    By referring to **one** example, explain how the writer's use of language creates a sense of despair.   **2**

31. By referring to this extract and to at least one other story by Crichton Smith, show how he uses word choice **and/or** symbolism to highlight an important message.   **8**

[Turn over

OR

Text 5 — Prose

If you choose this text you may not attempt a question on Prose in Section 2.

Read the extract below and then attempt the following questions.

Zimmerobics **by Anne Donovan**

So that was that. At 11am I assembled with the others in the dayroom. I knew most of their faces, but was surprised to see some of them wearing tracksuits and trainers. It hadn't occurred to me to ask what to wear and I didn't possess such things anyway, but somehow I felt out of place. It was like starting school and discovering that the others were wearing
5 school uniform and you weren't.

Cheryl bounced into the room, wearing a pair of trainers that made her feet look like a horse's hooves. Her hair was tied back with an emerald green band which matched her shimmering leotard and tights.

"I hope she doesn't need to go to the toilet in a hurry," muttered a voice behind me.

10 "Hi there. It's great to see so many of you here this morning. Now, take it at your own pace and if you feel uncomfortable or out of breath any time, stop for a wee rest. Enjoy!"

She switched on the music. We stood behind our Zimmers as she got us to stretch first one, then the other, arm, move our heads to each side, then stretch our legs. I heard a few creaking sounds but so far so good. We moved on to circling movements and, as the record
15 progressed, I felt an unaccustomed but pleasant tingling in my limbs.

"That was the warm-up. The next one's a bit faster."

The next record was a catchy tune about living in the YMCA. I couldn't keep up with the routine at first but, once we'd been through it a few times, I became quite proficient. We had to raise our right then our left arms to the Y and the M, then pause on the C and hold
20 our Zimmers as we bent both legs for the A. Then we marched (well, shuffled in most cases) round to the left, raised our left arms twice to the Y and the M (that was a bit tricky), paused at the C and kicked our left leg out to the A. During the verse we did some marching and a few kicks, then we repeated the chorus routine, this time moving to the right. At the end we clapped three times, boldly taking both hands off our Zimmer frames.

25 It was brilliant. I hadn't felt like this for years. My body was old and decrepit, but it still worked. I had been concentrating so hard on what I was doing I had forgotten the others, but now I looked round and saw their faces, flushed and smiling.

"You all did great. Give yourselves a round of applause." She clapped her hands above her head while we patted our hands together, slightly embarrassed.

30 "Same time next week," she called as we hirpled out of the dayroom, old once again.

The memory of the exercise class lingered on for the rest of the day, not just in my mind as I relived the routine, but in my bones and muscles. I thought I'd be sore and stiff but, surprisingly, I felt better, as though someone had oiled all the creaky old joints. There was a feeling in them which I suppose you would call an ache, but it was a pleasant ache, an
35 ache of life.

MARKS

Questions

32. Using your own words as far as possible, explain how Miss Knight's attitude to Zimmerobics changes over the extract. You should make **two** key points in your answer.

2

33. Look at lines 12—35.

   By referring to **one** example, explain how the writer's use of language makes clear the problems associated with old age.

2

34. Look again at lines 12—35.

   By referring to **two** examples, explain how the writer's use of language makes clear Miss Knight's feelings about exercise.

4

35. Look at the extract as a whole.

   By referring to **two** examples, explain how the writer's use of language creates humour.

4

36. By referring to this extract and to at least one other story, show how Donovan creates convincing characters.

8

[Turn over

SECTION 1 — SCOTTISH TEXT — 20 marks

PART C — SCOTTISH TEXT — POETRY

Text 1 — Poetry

If you choose this text you may not attempt a question on Poetry in Section 2.

Read the poem below and then attempt the following questions.

War Photographer **by Carol Ann Duffy**

In his darkroom he is finally alone
with spools of suffering set out in ordered rows.
The only light is red and softly glows,
as though this were a church and he
5   a priest preparing to intone a Mass.
Belfast. Beirut. Phnom Penh. All flesh is grass.

He has a job to do. Solutions slop in trays
beneath his hands, which did not tremble then
though seem to now. Rural England. Home again
10 to ordinary pain which simple weather can dispel,
to fields which don't explode beneath the feet
of running children in a nightmare heat.

Something is happening. A stranger's features
faintly start to twist before his eyes,
15 a half-formed ghost. He remembers the cries
of this man's wife, how he sought approval
without words to do what someone must
and how the blood stained into foreign dust.

A hundred agonies in black and white
20 from which his editor will pick out five or six
for Sunday's supplement. The reader's eyeballs prick
with tears between the bath and pre-lunch beers.
From the aeroplane he stares impassively at where
he earns his living and they do not care.

MARKS

Questions

37. Look at lines 1—6.

By referring to **one** example of word choice, explain how the poet suggests that the war photographer is like "a priest" in "church".

2

38. Look at lines 9—12.

By referring to **two** examples of language, explain how the poet makes it clear that the war photographer's home country is very different from the countries he visits.

4

39. Look at lines 13—18.

By referring to **two** examples of language, explain how the poet makes it clear that the war photographer has been strongly affected by his experiences.

4

40. Look at lines 19—24.

Using your own words as far as possible, explain **two** key ideas explored in the final stanza.

2

41. By referring to this poem and to at least one other by Duffy, show how the idea of people suffering painful experiences is a feature of her poetry.

8

[Turn over

OR

Text 2 — Poetry

If you choose this text you may not attempt a question on Poetry in Section 2.

Read the poem below and then attempt the following questions.

Trio by Edwin Morgan

Coming up Buchanan Street, quickly, on a sharp winter evening
a young man and two girls, under the Christmas lights —
The young man carries a new guitar in his arms,
the girl on the inside carries a very young baby,
5   and the girl on the outside carries a chihuahua.
And the three of them are laughing, their breath rises
in a cloud of happiness, and as they pass
the boy says, 'Wait till he sees this but!'
The chihuahua has a tiny Royal Stewart tartan coat like a teapot-
10   holder,
the baby in its white shawl is all bright eyes and mouth like favours
     in a fresh sweet cake,
the guitar swells out under its milky plastic cover, tied at the neck
     with silver tinsel tape and a brisk sprig of mistletoe.
15 Orphean sprig! Melting baby! Warm chihuahua!
The vale of tears is powerless before you.
Whether Christ is born, or is not born, you
put paid to fate, it abdicates
                   under the Christmas lights.
20 Monsters of the year
go blank, are scattered back,
can't bear this march of three.

—And the three have passed, vanished in the crowd
(yet not vanished, for in their arms they wind
25 the life of men and beasts, and music,
laughter ringing them round like a guard)
at the end of this winter's day.

MARKS

Questions

42. Look at lines 1—8.

By referring to **one** example of language, explain how the poet creates a sense of joy.   2

43. Look at lines 11—14.

By referring to **one** example of language, explain how the poet suggests the idea of innocence.   2

44. Look at lines 15—22.

By referring to **two** examples of language, explain how the poet makes it clear that the group of three represents a strong force.   4

45. Look at lines 23—27.

By referring to **two** examples of language, explain how the poet creates a positive ending to the poem.   4

46. By referring to this poem and to at least one other by Morgan, show how setting is an important feature of his poetry.   8

[Turn over

OR

Text 3 — Poetry

If you choose this text you may not attempt a question on Poetry in Section 2.

Read the poem below and then attempt the following questions.

Aunt Julia **by Norman MacCaig**

Aunt Julia spoke Gaelic
very loud and very fast.
I could not answer her —
I could not understand her.

5　She wore men's boots
when she wore any.
— I can see her strong foot,
stained with peat,
paddling with the treadle of the spinningwheel
10　while her right hand drew yarn
marvellously out of the air.

Hers was the only house
where I've lain at night
in the absolute darkness
15　of a box bed, listening to
crickets being friendly.

She was buckets
and water flouncing into them.
She was winds pouring wetly
20　round house-ends.
She was brown eggs, black skirts
and a keeper of threepennybits
in a teapot.

Aunt Julia spoke Gaelic
25　very loud and very fast.
By the time I had learned
a little, she lay
silenced in the absolute black
of a sandy grave
30　at Luskentyre. But I hear her still, welcoming me
with a seagull's voice
across a hundred yards
of peatscrapes and lazybeds
and getting angry, getting angry
35　with so many questions
unanswered.

MARKS

Questions

47. Look at lines 1—4.

    By referring to **one** example of language, explain how the poet creates a clear sense of frustration.

    2

48. Look at lines 5—23.

    By referring to **two** examples of language, explain how the poet makes clear what Aunt Julia represents.

    4

49. Look at lines 26—30 ("By the . . . Luskentyre").

    By referring to **two** examples of language, explain how the poet creates a sad tone.

    4

50. Look at lines 30—36 ("But I . . . unanswered").

    How effective do you find these lines as a conclusion to the poem? You should refer to **one** example from these lines, and to the language **and/or** ideas of the rest of the poem.

    2

51. By referring to this poem and to at least one other by MacCaig, show how being separated from people **and/or** things is an important idea in his poetry.

    8

[Turn over

OR

Text 4 — Poetry

If you choose this text you may not attempt a question on Poetry in Section 2.

Read the poem below and then attempt the following questions.

Bed by Jackie Kay

She is that guid tae me so she is
an Am a burden tae her, I know Am ur.
Stuck here in this big blastit bed
year in, year oot, ony saint wuid complain.

5   There's things she has tae dae fir me
A' wish she didnae huv tae dae.
Am her wean noo, wey ma great tent o' nappy,
an champed egg in a cup, an mashed tattie.

Aw the treats A' used tae gie her,
10   she's gieing me. A' dinny ken whit happened.
We dinny talk any mair. Whether it's jist
the blethers ha been plucked oot o' us

an Am here like some skinny chicken,
ma skin aw bubbles and dots and spots,
15   loose flap noo (an yet as a young wuman
A' took pride in ma guid smooth skin.)

Aw A' dae is sit an look oot this windae.
A've seen hale generations graw up
an simmer doon fray this same windae —
20   that's no seen a lick o' paint fir donkeys.

The Kerrs have disappeared, but the last
Campbells ur still here so Am telt —
tho' hauf the time A' dinny believe her:
A've no seen ony Campbell in a lang time.

25   My dochter says 'Awright mother?'
haunds me a thin broth or puried neep
an A say 'Aye fine,' an canny help
the great heaving sigh that comes oot

my auld loose lips, nor ma crabbit tut,
30   nor ma froon when A' pu' ma cardie tight
aroon ma shooders fir the night drawin in.
Am jist biding time so am ur.

Time is whit A' hauld between
the soft bits o' ma thumbs,
35   the skeleton underneath ma night goon;
aw the while the glaring selfish moon

lights up this drab wee prison.
A'll be gone and how wull she feel?
No that Am saying A' want her guilty.
40   No that Am saying Am no grateful.

Page twenty-four

MARKS

Questions

52. Look at lines 1—12.

By referring to **two** examples of language, explain how the poet makes it clear that the speaker is unhappy with her current situation.   4

53. Look at lines 13—20.

By referring to **two** examples of language, explain how the poet gives a clear impression of the negative aspects of old age.   4

54. Look at lines 21—31.

By referring to **one** example of language, explain how the poet suggests that the speaker's relationship with her daughter is problematic.   2

55. Look at lines 32—40.

Using your own words as far as possible, explain the speaker's thoughts about what her life has become. You should make **two** key points in your answer.   2

56. By referring to this poem and to at least one other by Kay, show how she explores important changes in people's lives.   8

[END OF SECTION 1]

[Turn over

SECTION 2 — CRITICAL ESSAY — 20 marks

Attempt ONE question from the following genres — Drama, Prose, Poetry, Film and Television Drama, or Language.

Your answer must be on a different genre from that chosen in Section 1.

You should spend approximately 45 minutes on this Section.

DRAMA

Answers to questions in this part should refer to the text and to such relevant features as characterisation, key scene(s), structure, climax, theme, plot, conflict, setting . . .

1. Choose a play in which there is conflict.

   Describe the conflict and by referring to the playwright's use of dramatic techniques, explain fully how the conflict develops.

2. Choose a play in which there is a scene that can be described as a turning point.

   Briefly describe what happens in this scene, and by referring to appropriate dramatic techniques, go on to explain why the scene is important to the play as a whole.

PROSE

Answers to questions in this part should refer to the text and to such relevant features as characterisation, setting, language, key incident(s), climax, turning point, plot, structure, narrative technique, theme, ideas, description . . .

3. Choose a novel **or** a short story **or** a work of non-fiction which deals with an important issue or theme.

   By referring to appropriate techniques, show how the issue or theme is explored.

4. Choose a novel **or** a short story **or** a work of non-fiction which has a memorable character/person, place or event.

   By referring to appropriate techniques, explain how the writer makes the character/person, place or event memorable.

POETRY

> *Answers to questions in this part should refer to the text and to such relevant features as word choice, tone, imagery, structure, content, rhythm, rhyme, theme, sound, ideas . . .*

5. Choose a poem which has a strong message.

    Consider the whole poem, and by referring to poetic techniques explain how the strong message is explored.

6. Choose a poem which creates a particular mood or atmosphere.

    By referring to poetic techniques, show how the poet creates this particular mood or atmosphere.

FILM AND TELEVISION DRAMA

> *Answers to questions in this part should refer to the text and to such relevant features as use of camera, key sequence, characterisation, mise-en-scène, editing, setting, music/sound, special effects, plot, dialogue . . .*

7. Choose a scene or a sequence from a film or TV drama* which has a powerful impact on the audience.

    By referring to appropriate techniques, explain how the director creates this impact.

8. Choose a film or TV drama* which explores an important issue.

    By referring to appropriate techniques, explain how the director presents the issue in the film/TV drama as a whole.

* "TV drama" includes a single play, a series or a serial.

[Turn over

LANGUAGE

> *Answers to questions in this part should refer to the text and to such relevant features as register, accent, dialect, slang, jargon, vocabulary, tone, abbreviation . . .*

9. Consider the use of persuasive language in one or more advertisements that you have studied.

    By referring to appropriate language techniques, explain how language is used effectively.

10. Consider the language used by two groups of people who are different in an important way. For example, they may be different in age, be from different places, or have different jobs.

    By referring to specific examples, explain how language differences are important.

[END OF SECTION 2]

[END OF QUESTION PAPER]

National
Qualifications
2018

X824/75/11

English
Reading for Understanding,
Analysis and Evaluation

MONDAY, 14 MAY

9:00 AM – 10:00 AM

Total marks — 30

Attempt ALL questions.

Write your answers clearly in the answer booklet provided. In the answer booklet you must clearly identify the question number you are attempting.

Use **blue** or **black** ink.

Before leaving the examination room you must give your answer booklet to the Invigilator; if you do not you may lose all the marks for this paper.

Why do cats love bookshops?

When I walk into my local bookshop, the first thing I do (after saying hi to the owners) is look for the shop cat, Tiny the Mini Master. Tiny is the photogenic spirit of the place who gives you approximately five seconds to impress him, otherwise he goes right back to sleep on that pile of nineteenth-century novels.

5 I understand the idea of people being either more for dogs or cats, I do. I also get the weird looks I've received for proudly stating that I'm for both, that I can relate to dogs and their wonderfully dumb, but fiercely loyal attitudes, as well as appreciate the way cats keep you in check by making you work for their love. But I can say without any doubt that bookshop cats represent the apex of domesticated pets.

10 If a bookshop is so fortunate as to have a cat on the premises during opening hours, you can bet that feline is co-owner, manager, security, and the abiding conscience of the place. Cats generally seem above it all — that's what I tend to like about them. Personally, I'm more like a dog, all stupid and excited about the smallest things, easy to read and always hungry. Cats, on the other hand, look right through you, force you to contemplate things; they just seem smarter than
15 they're letting on, as if they know everything but won't tell. So it makes sense to see so many of them navigating the stacks of dusty old hardcovers at used bookshops. But there's another, deeper reason cats make so much sense in bookshops — it's in their DNA.

'One cannot help wondering what the silent critic on the hearth-rug thinks of our strange conventions — the mystic Persian, whose ancestors were worshipped as gods, whilst we, their
20 masters and mistresses, grovelled in caves and painted our bodies blue,' the famous novelist Virginia Woolf wrote in the essay 'On a Faithful Friend'. Cats held a special place in ancient Egyptian society, to the point where if you even accidentally killed a cat, you'd be sentenced to death. Cats were often adorned with jewels, and fed meals that would make today's tinned cat food look like, well, tinned cat food. They were sometimes mummified (the grieving owners
25 shaved off their eyebrows as an act of mourning). Bastet, the deity representing protection, fertility, and motherhood, could turn herself into a cat, hence the popular idea that Egyptians worshipped them.

It's pretty obvious that cats haven't really moved on from the sort of treatment they received in the time of Pharaoh. They carry themselves in a stately manner and demand that you treat them
30 with a certain amount of reverence, letting you know if you're doing a good job of petting them, when they're ready for their meal, and making you aware of what they like and what displeases them. My cats certainly do. They love their comfy spots, and often give me a hard time when I try to make them move, shooting me a look, letting out a sad meow, and then instigating a showdown which almost always ends with me picking them up. And their favourite place in my
35 house? Among my books.

Egypt, where cats are believed to have been first domesticated, is also where the relationship with bookshops can be traced. While mainly used to keep rodents away from homes and crops, cats were trained to keep pests away from papyrus rolls which contained texts. Without cats, in fact, it's hard to imagine how Egyptian civilisation could have so successfully weathered the
40 diseases and famine caused by vermin — but also imagine the knowledge that might have been lost were it not for those four-legged protectors guarding the temples from tiny intruders.

Today, when we think of a cat chasing a mouse it's usually in some cartoonesque, Tom and Jerry sort of way. The dumb cat is always foiled by its tiny adversary, like we're supposed to forgive the little pests for gnawing on our possessions and spreading disease. It's unfair.

45 So how did they end up in bookshops? Look to Russia and a decree issued by Empress Elizabeth in 1745 for the 'best and biggest cats, capable of catching mice' to be sent to the Museum of St Petersburg to protect the treasures contained within from rats (the tradition lives on to the present day, with dozens of strays living in the basement of the museum). Not long after, in the early 1800s, with Europeans still sure that rats caused the Black Death (this idea has been recently
50 debunked, with scholars now believing that giant gerbils might be to blame), and rat catchers unable to stop rodents from overrunning filthy urban centres, the British government started to encourage libraries to keep cats in order to bring down populations of book-loving vermin. It made sense that bookshop owners would also employ the four-legged security guards to keep their shops free of pests. Cats were easy to find, and all you had to do was feed them as
55 compensation. And once cats were invited into bookshops, they never really left.

Cats are quiet and want to be left alone for the bulk of the day; they're animals that long for solitude, much like readers and writers. It began as a working relationship, but became something more than that, something deeper. Cats ultimately became integral to the bookshop experience, a small part of why you would rather go to your local shop than buy online. Sure, not every
60 bookshop has a cat prowling around; but in the ones that do, the cats are a big part of what makes these stores great (along with, you know, the booksellers and the comfortable places to sit and read).

Of course, if you asked a cat, he'd say he was the main attraction, but that's what you get from a species which once reached god-like status.

Jason Diamond, Literary Hub

MARKS

Total marks — 30
Attempt ALL Questions

1. Look at lines 1—4. Explain **in your own words** why 'the first thing' the writer does when he visits his local bookshop is to 'look for the shop cat, Tiny.'

    You should make **two** key points in your answer.   2

2. Look at lines 5—17. Identify, **in your own words** as far as possible, **five** positive points the writer makes about cats.   5

3. Look at lines 18—27. Identify, **in your own words** as far as possible, **four** ways in which cats 'held a special place' in the ancient world.   4

4. By referring to the sentence in lines 28—29 ('It's pretty obvious . . . of Pharaoh'), explain how it helps to provide a link between the writer's ideas at this point in the passage.   2

5. Look at lines 32—35 ('My cats . . . my books.'). Explain how **one** example of the writer's use of sentence structure makes it clear what cats prefer.   2

6. Look at lines 36—41. Explain how **two** examples of the writer's word choice makes it clear that cats played a very important part in preserving Egyptian writing.   4

7. Look at lines 42—44. Explain how **two** examples of language make it clear that the writer is defending cats here.   4

8. Look at lines 45—55. Summarise, **in your own words** as far as possible, how cats ended up in bookshops.

    You should make **five** key points in your answer.   5

9. Look at lines 56—64. Select any expression from these lines and explain how it contributes to the passage's effective conclusion.   2

[END OF QUESTION PAPER]

National Qualifications 2018

X824/75/12

English
Critical Reading

MONDAY, 14 MAY

10:20 AM – 11:50 AM

Total marks — 40

SECTION 1 — Scottish Text — 20 marks

Read an extract from a Scottish text you have previously studied.

Choose ONE text from either

Part A — Drama   Pages 2–7

or

Part B — Prose   Pages 8–17

or

Part C — Poetry   Pages 18–25

Attempt ALL the questions for your chosen text.

SECTION 2 — Critical Essay — 20 marks

Attempt ONE question from the following genres — Drama, Prose, Poetry, Film and Television Drama, or Language.

Your answer must be on a different genre from that chosen in Section 1.

You should spend approximately 45 minutes on each Section.

Write your answers clearly in the answer booklet provided. In the answer booklet you must clearly identify the question number you are attempting.

Use **blue** or **black** ink.

Before leaving the examination room you must give your answer booklet to the Invigilator; if you do not, you may lose all the marks for this paper.

SECTION 1 — SCOTTISH TEXT — 20 marks

PART A — SCOTTISH TEXT — DRAMA

Text 1 — Drama

If you choose this text you may not attempt a question on Drama in Section 2.

Read the extract below and then attempt the following questions.

***Bold Girls* by Rona Munro**

In this extract, Cassie, Marie and Nora have returned from their night out. They are in Marie's house discussing the events of the night.

NORA: (*drawing herself up*) Oh you'll be telling me a different tale in the morning! There's no end to your wild tales, Cassie! There's no end to them, Marie! (*She snatches up her drink and takes an angry gulp*) And I'd it all to do. I'd it all to put up with! Are you hearing me?

5   *Cassie doesn't look at Nora*

          (*Taking another gulp*) He's lost my remnant, Marie. He's lost it. I'd all the money saved, as good as paid. It's gone he says, gone. I'll never find a colour like that again. Months I'd been dreaming of the glow that would give my front room. Months. And he's lost it. I'll never have it the way I want it now. Never. (*She is*
10   *getting tearful in her turn*) My lovely wee room. It could be lovely, couldn't it, Marie?

MARIE: You'll get it right, Nora.

NORA: Well where will I ever find a colour like that again? Tell me that? (*Waiting for a response*) Cassie? I'm asking you!

15   CASSIE: (*looking up at Nora*) Good night, Mummy.

     Nora stares at her for a moment, then she nods

NORA: Well I'm going up the town tomorrow. I'm just going to go up the town and buy a piece of what I want. I'll get credit. I'll give them a false address and I'll get credit and I'll have my loose covers. And if you don't want to come and help
20   choose them, Cassie, you needn't sit on them.

     Nora exits

     Marie puts the gin bottle down in front of Cassie. Cassie helps herself to another drink

MARIE: (*quietly*) It'll tear the heart out of her, Cassie.

CASSIE: Mummy's heart is made of steel. She had to grow it that way.

25   *Marie reaches over and takes Michael's picture. She goes and rehangs it carefully*

          There's a waitress up that club will be walking round without her hair tomorrow if I can find her.

MARIE: You don't know it was her. There's people in and out of here all the time.

CASSIE: Who else would it be?

MARKS

30 MARIE: Well — if she's thieving round the club there'll be others sort her out before you do. (*She steps back to admire the picture*)

      CASSIE: How do you stand it here, Marie?

      MARIE: Sure where else would I go?

      CASSIE: How do you keep that smile on your face?

35 MARIE: Super-glue.

      CASSIE: There's not one piece of bitterness in you, is there?

      MARIE: Oh Cassie.

      CASSIE: You see, you're good. And I'm just wicked.

      MARIE: Aye you're a bold woman altogether.

40 CASSIE: Is it hard being good?

      MARIE: I took lessons.

Questions

1. Using your own words as far as possible, identify **four** things we learn about the main characters in this extract.   **4**

2. Look at lines 6–11.

   By referring to **two** examples of language, explain how the writer makes it clear that Nora is upset.   **4**

3. By referring to **two** examples from anywhere in this extract, explain how stage directions are used to create tension between characters.   **4**

4. By referring to this extract and to elsewhere in the play, show how the main characters are presented as being 'Bold Girls'.   **8**

[Turn over

OR

Text 2 — Drama

If you choose this text you may not attempt a question on Drama in Section 2.

Read the extract below and then attempt the following questions.

Sailmaker **by Alan Spence**

	BILLY:	Ah hear the boy's daein well at school.
	DAVIE:	Oh aye. He's clever. He'll get on.
	BILLY:	He'll get on a lot better if you screw the heid, right?
	DAVIE:	C'mon Billy, ah dae ma best. It's just . . .
5	BILLY:	Ah know it's hard on yer own an that . . .
	DAVIE:	Naw ye don't know. Naebody knows, unless they've been through it. (*Quieter*) Comin hame's the worst. The boy's oot playin. Hoose is empty. Gets on top of ye.
		The other night there, ah got this queer feelin. Ah felt as if aw the furniture an everythin was *watching* me. Sounds daft, eh? Maybe ah'm goin aff ma heid!
10	BILLY:	Bound tae take a while tae get over it.
	DAVIE:	If ah ever dae.

(*They cross to where* ALEC *is playing with yacht*)

	BILLY:	(To ALEC) How ye doin wee yin? What's this ye've got? (*Picks up yacht*)
	ALEC:	Used tae be Jackie's.
15	DAVIE:	Ah'm gonnae fix it up, when ah've got the time.
	ALEC:	Ye've been sayin that for weeks!
	BILLY:	Ah could paint it if ye like.
	ALEC:	Would ye?
20	BILLY:	Aye, sure. Should come up really nice. Ah'll take it away wi me. Get it done this week.
	ALEC:	This week!
	BILLY:	Nae bother.
	ALEC:	What colours will ye make it?
25	BILLY:	Ah think the hull has tae be white. Ah've got a nice white gloss at work. The keel ah could dae in blue. Maybe put a wee blue rim round the edge here. An ah think ah've got a light brown that would do just fine for the deck. That suit ye awright?
	ALEC:	Great!
	BILLY:	Ye won't even recognise it. It'll be like a brand new boat.
	ALEC:	It'll be dead real, eh?
30	BILLY:	It'll be that real we can aw sail away in it!

MARKS

DAVIE: Away tae Never Never Land!

BILLY: Right, ah'll be seein ye.

(*Takes yacht, exits*)

Questions

5. Look at lines 1—11.

    By referring to **two** examples of language, explain how the writer makes it clear that Davie is having a difficult time.   4

6. Look at lines 13—28.

    By referring to **two** examples of language, explain what we learn about Billy's character.   4

7. Look at lines 29—33.

    By referring to **one** example, explain how either Alec **or** Davie react to Billy's promise of fixing the yacht.   2

8. Using your own words as far as possible, explain why the yacht is important in this extract. You should make **two** key points.   2

9. By referring to this extract and to elsewhere in the play, show how family relationships are explored.   8

[Turn over

OR

Text 3 — Drama

If you choose this text you may not attempt a question on Drama in Section 2.

Read the extract below and then attempt the following questions.

***Tally's Blood* by Ann Marie Di Mambro**

	ROSINELLA:	You better watch these lassies. (*Franco scoffs*) Who is it anyway? Anybody I know?
	FRANCO:	(*Face lights up talking about her*) This is not 'anybody'. It's Bridget Devlin. You know her?
5	ROSINELLA:	(*Disapproving*) From the Auld Toon? Adam Devlin's lassie?
	FRANCO:	What if she is?
	ROSINELLA:	No harm to the lassie, Franco, but look at that family. Must be six or seven weans.
	FRANCO:	Eight.
10	ROSINELLA:	(*Shocked*) Eight weans! She keeps having them and she cannie even look after them right. And look at me! It's no fair, is it. Twelve years I've been married — and nothing. Me an Italian as well.
	FRANCO:	They're a great family, Rosinella. Really close.
	ROSINELLA:	You never met anybody in Italy?
15	FRANCO:	I wasn't looking.
	ROSINELLA:	I says to Massimo, I wouldn't be surprised if you come back engaged.
	FRANCO:	I told you, Rosinella, I've got someone.
	ROSINELLA:	You're surely no keen on this Scotch girl?
	FRANCO:	What if I am?
20	ROSINELLA:	Then she must be giving you something you can't get from an Italian girl. I'm telling you, you better watch yourself.
	FRANCO:	You know nothing about Bridget.
25	ROSINELLA:	Now you listen good to me, son. These Scotch girls, they're all the same. They just go out with you for one thing. Because your faither's got a shop and they think you've got money.
	FRANCO:	(*Indignant*) Thanks very much.
	ROSINELLA:	Alright. Alright. And because you're tall . . .
	FRANCO:	Good looking . . .
	ROSINELLA:	You're good fun to be with . . .
30	FRANCO:	. . . a good kisser, a good dancer . . .
	ROSINELLA:	Aye, but that's because you're Italian.

MARKS

FRANCO: Oh, they like that alright. All I have to do is say 'Ciao Bella' and they're all over me.

Lucia in from front shop.

35   Ciao Bella.

She jumps on his back for a piggyback.

See what I mean?

ROSINELLA: Listen — these girls. (*Lowers voice so Lucia won't hear*) Don't think I don't understand. You're no different from all the other Italian men. You're young,
40   you've got the warm blood. But it's one thing to play around with them, so long as you marry your own kind. You watch none of them catches you. That's the kind of thing they do here.

Questions

10. Look at lines 1—6.

     By referring to **two** examples of language, explain how the writer makes it clear that there is conflict between Franco and Rosinella.   4

11. Look at lines 7—13.

     (a) By referring to **one** example, explain how the writer demonstrates Rosinella's opinion of Bridget's family.   2

     (b) By referring to **one** example, explain how the writer demonstrates Franco's opinion of Bridget's family.   2

12. Look at lines 15—42.

     By referring to **two** examples of language, explain what is revealed about Franco's character.   4

13. By referring to this extract and to elsewhere in the play, show how the character of Rosinella is presented.   8

[Turn over

SECTION 1 — SCOTTISH TEXT — 20 marks

PART B — SCOTTISH TEXT — PROSE

Text 1 — Prose

If you choose this text you may not attempt a question on Prose in Section 2.

Read the extract below and then attempt the following questions.

***The Cone-Gatherers* by Robin Jenkins**

In this extract, Neil and Calum have been caught in a storm and take refuge in the summer house belonging to the Runcie-Campbell family. Calum has picked up a doll.

'Put it back, Calum,' he said.

'Would it be all right if I took it away and put a leg on it?' asked Calum eagerly. 'I would bring it back.'

'No, it would not. It would be stealing. Put it back. In any case, it's just a doll, fit for a wee
5 lassie. Put it back.'

Neil went over to attend to the fire.

'Get your jacket off, Calum,' he said, 'and hold it in front of the fire.'

As he spoke he was cautiously taking his own off. His shoulder joints were very stiff and sore.

10 'Do you know what I'm going to do?' he asked, as he was helping to take off his brother's jacket. 'I'm going to have a puff at that pipe you bought me in Lendrick.'

Calum was delighted. 'Is it a good pipe, Neil?'

'The best I ever had. It must have cost you a fortune.'

Calum laughed and shook his head. 'I'm not telling,' he said.

15 Neil was feeling in his pocket for the pipe when other noises outside were added to the drumming of the rain on the roof: a dog's bark, and voices.

As they stared towards the door, there came a scratching on it as of paws, and a whining. A minute later they heard the lady cry out 'Thank God!' and then a key rattled in the lock. The door was flung open to the accompaniment of the loudest peal of thunder since the
20 start of the storm.

From a safe distance the little dog barked at the trespassers. The lady had only a silken handkerchief over her head; her green tweed costume was black in places with damp. In the midst of the thunder she shouted: 'What is the meaning of this?' Though astonishment, and perhaps dampness, made her voice hoarse, it nevertheless was far more appalling to
25 the two men than any thunder. They could not meet the anger in her face. They gazed at her feet; her stockings were splashed with mud and her shoes had sand on them.

Neil did not know what to do or say. Every second of silent abjectness was a betrayal of himself, and especially of his brother who was innocent. All his vows of never again being ashamed of Calum were being broken. His rheumatism tortured him, as if coals from the
30 stolen fire had been pressed into his shoulders and knees; but he wished that the pain was twenty times greater to punish him as he deserved. He could not lift his head; he tried, so that he could meet the lady's gaze at least once, no matter how scornful and contemptuous it was; but he could not. A lifetime of frightened submissiveness held it down.

MARKS

Suddenly he realised that Calum was speaking.

35 'It's not Neil's fault, lady,' he was saying. 'He did it because I was cold and wet.'

'For God's sake,' muttered the lady, and Neil felt rather than saw how she recoiled from Calum, as if from something obnoxious, and took her children with her.

Questions

14. Look at lines 1—14.

     By referring to **two** examples, explain what we learn about the relationship between Calum and Neil.   4

15. Look at lines 15—20.

     By referring to **two** examples of language, explain how the writer creates tension.   4

16. Look at lines 27—37.

     By referring to **two** examples of language, explain how Neil feels at this point.   4

17. By referring to this extract and to elsewhere in the novel, show how **one** interesting character is created.   8

[Turn over

OR

Text 2 — Prose

If you choose this text you may not attempt a question on Prose in Section 2.

Read the extract below and then attempt the following questions.

The Testament of Gideon Mack by James Robertson

She put the car into first gear and drove off, spraying my legs with gravel. I half-thought of driving after her, but saw it was futile. She was in no mood to listen. She thought I was ill, that I had invented the whole thing about the Stone. But I knew I wasn't ill. She'd panicked because I'd said I loved her, and because she loved me too. *That* was what frightened her.

5   A crisis was upon me. I was sweating, seething with energy. If I didn't do something the energy would burst out of me and leave me wrecked on the floor. My left arm was twitching as if in contact with an electric fence. I wanted to go to the Stone, yet at the same time was afraid to go. It seemed to me that the Stone had provoked this crisis, had engineered it in some way. I paced round the manse, in and out of every room, up and
10   down the stairs. I'd just decided to get changed and head off for a long run, to try to calm down, when the bell rang again. I thought Elsie must have come back and rushed to the front door. A car had pulled up in the drive, but not Elsie's. It was Lorna Sprott.

'Gideon,' Lorna said. 'I've been at the museum. I missed the exhibition opening but I've had a good look round.' Something in my expression stopped her. 'Is this an awkward
15   moment?'

'Actually, I was about to go for a run.'

'You wouldn't like to come for a walk instead? I've got Jasper in the car. I was thinking we might go to the Black Jaws.'

I opened my mouth to make an excuse, but she didn't notice.

20   'The exhibition surprised me,' she said. 'I didn't think it would be my cup of tea at all, and I can't say I understood everything, but it was quite thought-provoking. I saw old Menteith's study and listened to you reading while I was looking down through that window. That's what put me in mind to go to the Black Jaws, the real place. I haven't been there for ages, and Jasper could do with a change from the beach.'

25   She looked pleadingly at me. How could I resist? Lorna stood on the step, inexorable and solid, and I knew I'd never get rid of her. Even if I slammed the door in her face she wouldn't leave me alone. I imagined her scraping and chapping at the windows until I let her in. 'Wait a minute,' I said, and went to get my boots and a jacket.

Perhaps I was meant to go for a walk with Lorna, to talk to her about what was going on.
30   Perhaps the Stone was wielding some strange power over events and had brought her to my door at this moment. In the minute or two it took me to get ready I made a decision. I would go with Lorna to the Black Jaws and, depending on how things went, I would swear her to secrecy, take her to Keldo Woods, and show her the Stone. I could trust her thus far, I knew. If Lorna acknowledged that the Stone existed, then I would know I was neither
35   hallucinating nor mad and I would go to Elsie and John. I would confront them with the misery and mockery of our lives and ask them to have the courage, with me, to change them. If, on the other hand, Lorna could not see the Stone, then I would have to admit that what Elsie had said was true, that I needed help.

40 I didn't know, as I locked the manse door and got into Lorna's car, that I wouldn't be back for nearly a week. Nor could I have foreseen that I would return utterly transformed. Nor indeed, as I strapped myself in and gritted my teeth against Lorna's terrible driving, and was greeted by Jasper's happy squeals and licks from the back seat, could I have guessed that it would not be Lorna who would trigger what happened next, but her dog.

Questions

18. Look at lines 5—12.

    By referring to **two** examples of language, explain how the writer creates tension. 4

19. Look at lines 13—24.

    By referring to **one** example, explain what we learn about the character of Lorna. 2

20. Look at lines 25—38.

    Using your own words as far as possible, identify **two** reasons why Gideon decides to go to the Black Jaws with Lorna. 2

21. Look at lines 39—43.

    By referring to **two** examples of language, explain how the writer makes this moment seem dramatic. 4

22. By referring to this extract and to elsewhere in the novel, show how setting is an important feature. 8

[Turn over

OR

Text 3 — Prose

If you choose this text you may not attempt a question on Prose in Section 2.

Read the extract below and then attempt the following questions.

***Kidnapped* by Robert Louis Stevenson**

In this extract, David Balfour and Alan Breck Stewart are escaping through the heather after spending some time with Cluny Macpherson.

At last, upon the other side of Loch Errocht, going over a smooth, rushy place, where the walking was easy, he could bear it no longer, and came close to me.

'David,' says he, 'this is no way for two friends to take a small accident. I have to say that I'm sorry; and so that's said. And now if you have anything, ye'd better say it.'

5 'O,' says I, 'I have nothing.'

He seemed disconcerted; at which I was meanly pleased.

'No,' said he, with rather a trembling voice, 'but when I say I was to blame?'

'Why, of course, ye were to blame,' said I, coolly; 'and you will bear me out that I have never reproached you.'

10 'Never,' says he; 'but ye ken very well that ye've done worse. Are we to part? Ye said so once before. Are ye to say it again? There's hills and heather enough between here and the two seas, David; and I will own I'm no very keen to stay where I'm no wanted.'

This pierced me like a sword, and seemed to lay bare my private disloyalty.

'Alan Breck!' I cried; and then: 'Do you think I am one to turn my back on you in your chief
15 need? You dursn't say it to my face. My whole conduct's there to give the lie to it. It's true, I fell asleep upon the muir; but that was from weariness, and you do wrong to cast it up to me —'

'Which is what I never did,' said Alan.

'But aside from that,' I continued, 'what have I done that you should even me to dogs by
20 such a supposition? I never yet failed a friend, and it's not likely I'll begin with you. There are things between us that I can never forget, even if you can.'

'I will only say this to ye, David,' said Alan, very quietly, 'that I have long been owing ye my life, and now I owe ye money. Ye should try to make that burden light for me.'

This ought to have touched me, and in a manner it did, but the wrong manner. I felt I was
25 behaving badly; and was now not only angry with Alan, but angry with myself in the bargain; and it made me the more cruel.

'You asked me to speak,' said I. 'Well, then, I will. You own yourself that you have done me a disservice; I have had to swallow an affront: I have never reproached you, I never named the thing till you did. And now you blame me,' cried I, 'because I cannae laugh and sing as
30 if I was glad to be affronted. The next thing will be that I'm to go down upon my knees and thank you for it! Ye should think more of others, Alan Breck. If ye thought more of others, ye would perhaps speak less about yourself; and when a friend that likes you very well has passed over an offence without a word, you would be blithe to let it lie, instead of making it a stick to break his back with. By your own way of it, it was you that was to blame; then
35 it shouldnae be you to seek the quarrel.'

MARKS

'Aweel,' said Alan, 'say nae mair.'

And we fell back into our former silence; and came to our journey's end, and supped, and lay down to sleep, without another word.

Questions

23. Look at lines 1—9.

    By referring to **two** examples, explain how the writer makes clear the conflict between Alan and David.

    4

24. Look at lines 13—21.

    By referring to **two** examples of language, explain how the writer reveals David's anger.

    4

25. Look at lines 10—38.

    By referring to **two** examples, explain **two** things we learn about the character of Alan.

    4

26. By referring to this extract and to elsewhere in the novel, show how the writer explores the theme of friendship.

    8

[Turn over

OR

Text 4 — Prose

If you choose this text you may not attempt a question on Prose in Section 2.

Read the extract below and then attempt the following questions.

The Red Door by Iain Crichton Smith

Murdo stared at the door and as he looked at it he seemed to be drawn inside it into its deep caves with all sorts of veins and passages. It was like a magic door out of the village but at the same time it pulsed with a deep red light which made it appear alive. It was all very odd and very puzzling, to think that a red door could make such a difference to house
5 and moors and streams.

Solid and heavy he stood in front of it in his wellingtons, scratching his head. But the red door was not a mirror and he couldn't see himself in it. Rather he was sucked into it as if it were a place of heat and colour and reality. But it was different and it was his.

It was true that the villagers when they woke would see it and perhaps make fun of it, and
10 would advise him to repaint it. They might not even want him in the village if he insisted on having a red door. Still they could all have red doors if they wanted to. Or they could hunt him out of the village.

Hunt him out of the village? He paused for a moment, stunned by the thought. It had never occurred to him that he could leave the village, especially at his age, forty-six. But then
15 other people had left the village and some had prospered though it was true that many had failed. As for himself, he could work hard, he had always done so. And perhaps he had never really belonged to the village. Perhaps his belonging had been like the Hallowe'en mask. If he were a true villager would he like the door so much? Other villagers would have been angry if their door had been painted red in the night, their anger reflected in the red
20 door, but he didn't feel at all angry, in fact he felt admiration that someone should actually have thought of this, should actually have seen the possibility of a red door, in a green and black landscape.

He felt a certain childlikeness stirring within him as if he were on Christmas day stealing barefooted over the cold red linoleum to the stocking hanging at the chimney, to see if
25 Santa Claus had come in the night while he slept.

Having studied the door for a while and having had a long look round the village which was rousing itself to a new day, repetitive as all the previous ones, he turned into the house. He ate his breakfast and thinking carefully and joyously and having washed the dishes he set off to see Mary though in fact it was still early.

30 His wellingtons creaked among the sparkling frost. Its virginal new diamonds glittered around him, millions of them. Before he knocked on her door he looked at his own door from a distance. It shone bravely against the frost and the drab patches without frost or snow. There was pride and spirit about it. It had emerged out of the old and the habitual, brightly and vulnerably. It said, 'Please let me live my own life.' He knocked on the door.

MARKS

Questions

27. Look at lines 1—8.

    By referring to **two** examples of language, explain how the writer suggests that the red door is unusual.   **4**

28. Look at lines 9—22.

    Using your own words as far as possible, explain Murdo's reaction to the door. You should make **two** key points in your answer.   **2**

29. Look at lines 23—29.

    By referring to **one** example of language, explain how the writer suggests a fresh start for Murdo.   **2**

30. Look at lines 30—34.

    By referring to **two** examples of language, explain how the writer creates a positive mood or atmosphere.   **4**

31. By referring to this extract and to at least one other story by Crichton Smith, show how an important theme is explored.   **8**

[Turn over

OR

Text 5 — Prose

If you choose this text you may not attempt a question on Prose in Section 2.

Read the extract below and then attempt the following questions.

Away in a Manger **by Anne Donovan**

'Naw. Are you cauld?'

'Just ma nose.'

She covered it wi her white mitt.

A vision of warmth, a fire, a mug of hot tea rose afore Sandra's eyes.

5 'We could come back and see the lights another night.'

'Naw, Mammy, naw, we cannae go hame noo, we're nearly there, you promised . . .'

'All right, we'll go. Ah just thought you were too cauld.'

Amy had been gaun on aboot the lights for weeks; at least this would get it ower and done wi. God, she was sick of it all, specially the extra hours in the shop. Every Christmas they
10 opened longer and longer. Late-night shoppers, trippin ower wan another tae buy presents that'd be returned on Boxin Day, everybody in a bad mood, trachled wi parcels. And those bloody Christmas records playin non-stop. The extra hours meant extra money, right enough, and it wouldnae be so bad if they'd only tell you in advance, but see if that old bag of a supervisor sidled up tae her once more wi her 'Could you just do an extra couple of
15 hours tonight, Sandra?' Wanny these days she'd hit her ower the heid wi a gift-wrapped basket of Fruits of Nature toiletries.

No the night, though.

'Awful sorry, Linda. Ah'm takin Amy tae see the lights in George Square. Ma neighbour's gaun late-night shoppin so she'll bring her in tae meet me.'

20 'Amy'll love that.'

Sandra was foldin a shelf of red sweaters when Amy came intae the shop, wearin her new coat. She adored that coat, specially the hood, which had a white fur-fabric ruff round the edge. When she'd first got it she walked aboot the hoose in it wi the hood up and Sandra could hardly persuade her tae take it off at bedtime. It had been dear, too much really, but
25 Sandra always wanted Amy tae have nice things, she looked so good in them. She was a beautiful child, everybody said so; even the old bag.

'What a pretty wee girl you are. Oh, she's got gorgeous curls, Sandra.'

She pressed a coin intae Amy's haund.

'That'll buy you some sweeties, pet.'

30 'What do you say, Amy?'

'Thank you very much.'

Amy placed the coin carefully inside her mitt.

They turned the corner and the cauld evaporated. The square shimmerin wi light, brightness sharp against the gloomy street. Trees frosted wi light. Lights shaped intae
35 circles and flowers, like the plastic jewellery sets wee lassies love. Lights switchin on and off in a mad rhythm ae their ain, tryin tae look like bells ringin and snow fallin. Reindeer and Santas, holly, ivy, robins, all bleezin wi light. Amy gazed at them, eyes shinin.

MARKS

Questions

32. Look at lines 1–7.

    By referring to **one** example, explain how the writer's use of language makes it clear that Sandra is not very enthusiastic about the trip to see the lights.

    2

33. Look at lines 8–16.

    By referring to **two** examples, explain how the writer's use of language makes clear Sandra's feelings about the Christmas season.

    4

34. Look at lines 17–31.

    Using your own words as far as possible, explain Sandra's attitude towards her daughter, Amy, at this point in the story. You should make **two** key points in your answer.

    2

35. Look at lines 32–37.

    By referring to **two** examples, explain how the writer's use of language creates a magical atmosphere.

    4

36. By referring to this extract and to at least one other story by Donovan, show how important relationships are explored.

    8

[Turn over

SECTION 1 — SCOTTISH TEXT — 20 marks

PART C — SCOTTISH TEXT — POETRY

Text 1 — Poetry

If you choose this text you may not attempt a question on Poetry in Section 2.

Read the extract below and then attempt the following questions.

Mrs Midas **by Carol Ann Duffy**

It was late September. I'd just poured a glass of wine, begun
to unwind, while the vegetables cooked. The kitchen
filled with the smell of itself, relaxed, its steamy breath
gently blanching the windows. So I opened one,
5 then with my fingers wiped the other's glass like a brow.
He was standing under the pear tree snapping a twig.

Now the garden was long and the visibility poor, the way
the dark of the ground seems to drink the light of the sky,
but that twig in his hand was gold. And then he plucked
10 a pear from a branch — we grew Fondante d'Automne —
and it sat in his palm like a light bulb. On.
I thought to myself, Is he putting fairy lights in the tree?

He came into the house. The doorknobs gleamed.
He drew the blinds. You know the mind; I thought of
15 the Field of the Cloth of Gold and of Miss Macready.
He sat in that chair like a king on a burnished throne.
The look on his face was strange, wild, vain. I said,
What in the name of God is going on? He started to laugh.

I served up the meal. For starters, corn on the cob.
20 Within seconds he was spitting out the teeth of the rich.
He toyed with his spoon, then mine, then with the knives, the forks.
He asked where was the wine. I poured with a shaking hand,
a fragrant, bone-dry white from Italy, then watched
as he picked up the glass, goblet, golden chalice, drank.

MARKS

Questions

37. Look at lines 1—6.

    By referring to **two** examples of language, explain how the writer creates a calm mood.

    4

38. Look at lines 7—12.

    By referring to **two** examples of language, explain how the writer makes it clear that the speaker feels some uncertainty.

    4

39. Look at lines 13—24.

    By referring to **two** examples of language, explain how the writer makes it clear that something dramatic is now happening.

    4

40. By referring to this extract and to at least one other poem by Duffy, show how the poet creates interesting characters.

    8

[Turn over

OR

Text 2 — Poetry

If you choose this text you may not attempt a question on Poetry in Section 2.

Read the poem below and then attempt the following questions.

***Slate* by Edwin Morgan**

There is no beginning. We saw Lewis
laid down, when there was not much but thunder
and volcanic fires; watched long seas plunder
faults; laughed as Staffa cooled. Drumlins blue as
5　bruises were grated off like nutmegs; bens,
and a great glen, gave a rough back we like
to think the ages must streak, surely strike,
seldom stroke, but raised and shaken, with tens
of thousands of rains, blizzards, sea-poundings
10　shouldered off into night and memory.
Memory of men! That was to come. Great
in their empty hunger these surroundings
threw walls to the sky, the sorry glory
of a rainbow. Their heels kicked flint, chalk, slate.

MARKS

Questions

41.   Look at lines 1—5.

By referring to **two** examples, explain how the poet's use of language suggests the power and/or violence of the island's creation.   4

42.   Look at lines 6—10.

By referring to **two** examples, explain how the poet's use of language develops your understanding of the island.   4

43.   Look at lines 11—14.

By referring to **two** examples of language, explain how the poet gives a clear impression of change.   4

44.   By referring to this poem and to at least one other by Morgan, show how an important theme is explored.   8

[Turn over

OR

Text 3 — Poetry

If you choose this text you may not attempt a question on Poetry in Section 2.

Read the poem below and then attempt the following questions.

Memorial **by Norman MacCaig**

Everywhere she dies. Everywhere I go she dies.
No sunrise, no city square, no lurking beautiful mountain
but has her death in it.
The silence of her dying sounds through
5 the carousel of language, it's a web
on which laughter stitches itself. How can my hand
clasp another's when between them
is that thick death, that intolerable distance?

She grieves for my grief. Dying, she tells me
10 that bird dives from the sun, that fish
leaps into it. No crocus is carved more gently
than the way her dying
shapes my mind. — But I hear, too,
the other words,
15 black words that make the sound
of soundlessness, that name the nowhere
she is continuously going into.

Ever since she died
she can't stop dying. She makes me
20 her elegy. I am a walking masterpiece,
a true fiction
of the ugliness of death.
I am her sad music.

MARKS

Questions

45. Look at the poem as a whole.

    Using your own words as far as possible, explain **two** ways in which the woman's death has affected the speaker.

    2

46. Look at lines 1—8.

    By referring to **two** examples of language, explain how the strong impact of the woman's death is made clear.

    4

47. Look at lines 9—15.

    By referring to **two** examples of language, explain how the poet suggests that the woman still seems close.

    4

48. Select an expression from lines 19—23 ('She makes me . . . sad music.'), and explain how it helps to contribute to an effective ending to the poem.

    2

49. By referring to this poem and to at least one other by MacCaig, show how the poet uses language to explore important experiences.

    8

[Turn over

OR

Text 4 — Poetry

If you choose this text you may not attempt a question on Poetry in Section 2.

Read the extract below and then attempt the following questions.

Gap Year **by Jackie Kay**

I remember your Moses basket before you were born.
I'd stare at the fleecy white sheet for days, weeks,
willing you to arrive, hardly able to believe
I would ever have a real baby to put in the basket.

 5 I'd feel the mound of my tight tub of a stomach,
and you moving there, foot against my heart,
elbow in my ribcage, turning, burping, awake, asleep.
One time I imagined I felt you laugh.

I'd play you Handel's *Water Music* or Emma Kirkby
10 singing Pergolesi. I'd talk to you, my close stranger,
call you Tumshie, ask when you were coming to meet me.
You arrived late, the very hot summer of eighty-eight.

You had passed the due date string of eights,
and were pulled out with forceps, blue, floury,
15 on the fourteenth of August on Sunday afternoon.
I took you home on Monday and lay you in your basket.

Now, I peek in your room and stare at your bed
hardly able to imagine you back in there sleeping,
Your handsome face — soft, open. Now you are eighteen,
20 six foot two, away, away in Costa Rica, Peru, Bolivia.

I follow your trails on my *Times Atlas*:
from the Caribbean side of Costa Rica to the Pacific,
the baby turtles to the massive leatherbacks.
Then on to Lima, to Cuzco. Your grandfather

25 rings: 'Have you considered altitude sickness,
Christ, he's sixteen thousand feet above sea level.'
Then to the lost city of the Incas, Machu Picchu,
Where you take a photograph of yourself with the statue

of the original Tupac. You are wearing a Peruvian hat.
30 Yesterday in Puno before catching the bus for Copacabana,
you suddenly appear on a webcam and blow me a kiss,
you have a new haircut; your face is grainy, blurry.

MARKS

Questions

50. Look at lines 1—4.

    By referring to **one** example of language, explain how the poet creates a mood of excitement.

    2

51. Look at lines 5—12.

    By referring to **two** examples of language, explain how the poet suggests a strong bond between mother and baby.

    4

52. Look at lines 17—32.

    (a) By referring to **two** examples of language, explain how the poet makes clear the mother's feelings about her son being away.

    4

    (b) By referring to **one** example of language, explain how the grandfather reveals a different point of view.

    2

53. By referring to this extract and to at least one other poem by Kay, show how setting is an important feature.

    8

[END OF SECTION 1]

[Turn over

SECTION 2 — CRITICAL ESSAY — 20 marks

Attempt ONE question from the following genres — Drama, Prose, Poetry, Film and Television Drama, or Language.

Your answer must be on a different genre from that chosen in Section 1.

You should spend approximately 45 minutes on this Section.

DRAMA

Answers to questions in this part should refer to the text and to such relevant features as characterisation, key scene(s), structure, climax, theme, plot, conflict, setting . . .

1. Choose a play in which the writer creates an interesting character.

   By referring to appropriate techniques, explain how the writer makes this character interesting.

2. Choose a play which explores an important theme.

   By referring to appropriate techniques, explain how this theme is explored.

PROSE

Answers to questions in this part should refer to the text and to such relevant features as characterisation, setting, language, key incident(s), climax, turning point, plot, structure, narrative technique, theme, ideas, description . . .

3. Choose a novel **or** short story **or** a work of non-fiction which deals with a significant event or experience or issue.

   Give a brief account of the significant event or experience or issue. By referring to appropriate techniques, explain how it is important to the text as a whole.

4. Choose a novel **or** short story in which there is a character you feel strongly about.

   By referring to appropriate techniques, explain how the author creates this reaction in you.

POETRY

> *Answers to questions in this part should refer to the text and to such relevant features as word choice, tone, imagery, structure, content, rhythm, rhyme, theme, sound, ideas . . .*

5. Choose a poem which explores an aspect of human experience.

   By referring to poetic techniques, explain how this aspect of human experience is explored.

6. Choose a poem which makes effective use of setting.

   By referring to poetic techniques, explain how the setting adds to your appreciation of the poem as a whole.

FILM AND TELEVISION DRAMA

> *Answers to questions in this part should refer to the text and to such relevant features as use of camera, key sequence, characterisation, mise-en-scène, editing, setting, music/sound, special effects, plot, dialogue . . .*

7. Choose a film **or** TV drama* which has a memorable character.

   By referring to appropriate techniques, explain how the director makes the character memorable throughout the film or TV drama.

8. Choose a scene or sequence from a film **or** TV drama* in which setting is an important feature.

   By referring to appropriate techniques, explain how the director presents the setting in this scene or sequence.

* 'TV drama' includes a single play, a series or a serial.

[Turn over

LANGUAGE

Answers to questions in this part should refer to the text and to such relevant features as register, accent, dialect, slang, jargon, vocabulary, tone, abbreviation . . .

9. Choose an example of language which aims to persuade you to agree with a particular point of view, **or** to buy a product, **or** to influence your behaviour.

   By referring to specific examples, explain how persuasive language is used effectively.

10. Choose an example of language used by a group of people from the same place, **or** with the same job, **or** of the same age, **or** who have shared similar experiences.

   By referring to specific examples, explain the features of this language.

[END OF SECTION 2]

[END OF QUESTION PAPER]

NATIONAL 5

Answers

NATIONAL 5 ENGLISH
2016

READING FOR UNDERSTANDING, ANALYSIS AND EVALUATION

1. Any two points for 1 mark each.

    Glosses of:

    - "follow in the footsteps of Diana Ross and Whitney Houston" e.g. she was a great (female) singer/star too

    - "belt out" e.g. give a powerful delivery

    - "the voice of Elsa"/"the most successful animated film …" e.g. she was the singer of the hit film/song

    - "ubiquitous" e.g. the song was heard everywhere (accept e.g. "was well known")

    - "Oscar-winning" e.g. the song was critically acclaimed

    - "more than three million copies sold" e.g. the song was (very) popular/profitable

    - "(more than passing) acquaintance" e.g. she has (good) experience "with anthems" e.g. of important/ highly-regarded songs

2. 1 mark for reference; 1 mark for comment.

    - "stratospheric" e.g. suggests signal/immense/far-reaching/heightened achievement/out of this world

    - "(takings of more than) £800 million" OR "it's No 5 in the all-time list of highest-grossing films" OR uses statistics e.g. to show that the film has made a great deal of money

    - uses parenthesis to include (significant) statistics/ evidence

    - "has elevated her" e.g. she has achieved greater prominence

    - "into a new league" e.g. into a different (superior) context

3. Any five points.

    Glosses of:

    - "she has clearly been reprimanded" e.g. they have a system of discipline/control

    - "by the Disney suits" e.g. they are conventionally dressed (ie reference to appearance)

    - "by the Disney suits" e.g. conservative/corporate/ faceless (ie reference to attitude/mindset)

    - "Apparently I spoke out of turn" e.g. they disliked dissent

    - "Disney doesn't have sequels, (so it would be a first if there was one)" e.g. they don't (usually) produce follow-up films

    - "stage show" OR "six-minute short" OR "new song" indicates e.g. (commercial) versatility

    - "(much) mooted" e.g. Disney is the centre of speculation

    - "the Disney people keep things close to their chests" OR "tight-lipped" e.g. they are secretive/they say little

    - "happy to milk the commercial opportunities" OR "enjoyed a mighty bump" e.g. they take pleasure in exploiting/maximising the financial gain

4. 1 mark for reference; 1 mark for comment (×2).

    - "There to be shot at" e.g. suggests people's readiness to denigrate OR (image of) "shot at" illustrates e.g. the critics' aggression/hostility/targeting

    - "criticised" e.g. indicates open to negative comment

    - "failing to hit a high note" e.g. suggest harshness of criticism

    - parenthetical insertion (of "singing in sub-zero temperatures") e.g. serves to highlight the point

    - substance of "sub-zero temperatures" e.g. adverse conditions

    - "still some who noticed the odd flat note" e.g. suggests (excessive) vigilance of audience/inability to please everyone

    - "The unnerving" e.g. it is scary

    - "proximity" e.g. the footballers are close

    - "of several dozen" e.g. there are many of them

    - "hulking (American footballers)" OR "huge" e.g. they are very big/intimidating

    - "strong presence (these athletes have)" e.g. they have an aura/charisma

    - "you're this one woman, singing on her own" e.g. she was alone/an outnumbered female

    - "(they're so …) daunting" e.g. (the men are) intimidating

    - use of ellipsis suggests she wants to be precise in her own comments/provides a dramatic pause/ emphasises "daunting"

5. Any one pair OR two correct selections covering different directions.

    - "One woman" looks back to "one woman" OR "on her own" OR the idea of isolation

    - "squad of men" looks back to "several dozen hulking" OR "huge" OR "American footballers" OR the idea of male physical presence

    - "Frozen" looks forward to "Disney animation"

    - "a feminist breakthrough" looks forward to (idea of) "The first … to be directed … by a woman" OR "love … between two sisters" OR "not because some Prince Charming is saving the day"

    - "One woman opposite a squad of men" (accept paraphrase) looks back to the isolation of Idina Menzel

    - information before colon looks back information after colon looks forward

6. 1 mark for reference; 1 mark for comment (×2).

    - "heroine" e.g. strength of character

    - "subtle" e.g. not straightforward

    - "conflicted" e.g. has contradictory emotions/internal battles/complications

    - "sorceress" e.g. supernatural

    - "struggling to control her powers" e.g. has difficulties with her abilities

    - "she keeps [Anna] at a distance" e.g. deliberately remote

    - "for fear of turning her into a popsicle" e.g. she wields (potentially harmful) power

- "(grandiose) sulks" e.g. is (spectacularly) moody
- "emo (princess)" e.g. alternative/sensitive/of dark mind or appearance/saturnine
- "(definitely) complicated" e.g. (undeniably) complex
- "not stereotypes" e.g. not predictable/what is conventionally expected

7. • her sister's company (beautifully) encapsulated key ideas of the films
   - **OR** Travolta's error heightened her profile
   - **OR** the song was up for (and won) an (top) award — "Oscar" may be lifted and she got to sing it

8. It is possible to gain full marks through examination of one linguistic aspect.

   Sentence structure:
   - long compared to short sentences **OR** appropriate contrasting references shows complexity compared to simplicity

   Tone:
   - appropriate contrasting references e.g. "several zeitgeist-y things across different generations"/"people who are trying to find themselves" compared with "one more (burning) question"/"No I do not!" shows formality/seriousness compared to lightness/humour/vehemence

   Word choice:
   - "zeitgeist-y" **OR** "resonate" compared to "Does she have her own Elsa dress" shows the difference between difficulty and simplicity
   - "proud" and "much to learn" exhibits the difference between self-esteem and humility
   - "Rent to Wicked" **OR** "Glee to Frozen" illustrates then and now
   - "Frozen" and "burning". Comment must show understanding these are antonyms
   - "certainly aware" and "I have as much to learn myself". Comment must show understanding these are antonymous

9. *Any five from:*

Reference to	Glossed by (eg)
"I spoke out of turn"	She can be forthright/impulsive
"I'd have to play Elsa's mother, probably" or "she laughs"	She has a (self-deprecating) sense of humour
"she sounds slightly disappointed"	She likes to be the star/centre of attention/is self-centred
Despite criticisms	She shows persistence
"they're … daunting"	She can be intimidated
"not because some Prince Charming is saving the day"	She is assertive/feminist (accept slang)
"It was Cara whom Menzel took as her date"	She is close to/fond of her sister/caring
"wincingly"	She is modest/embarrassed by her sister's admiration

Reference to	Glossed by (eg)
"she … recognises … Travolta's slip"	She is perceptive/realistic
"her conversation is a mix of Broadway-speak"	She can be/is shrewd enough to adapt to her environment/use platitudes
"battled-hardened"	She is tough/resilient
"ambition"	She has aspirations
"aware of the value of appearing"	She is shrewd/pragmatic
"I'm proud of that"	She relishes fans' identification with her
"I have as much to learn myself"	She is modest/self-aware
"I don't look that good as a blonde"	She is modest NB please don't credit 'modest' twice
"she'd also quite enjoy ruling over her own wintry kingdom"	She enjoys power/dominance/prominence

CRITICAL READING

SECTION 1 — SCOTTISH TEXT

PART A — DRAMA — *Bold Girls* by Rona Munro

1. Any three key points for 1 mark each.

   Candidates are expected to use their own words.

   Possible answers include:
   - Deirdre confronts Marie about the truth about Michael (her father)
   - Marie tries to avoid telling her the truth
   - Marie (loses her temper) and destroys the photograph of Michael
   - Marie sees Deirdre's bruises and asks about them
   - there is temporary physical closeness between the women
   - the women start to face up to the truth about Michael (and his affairs)
   - there is an increasing sense of understanding between the women by the end of the extract

2. 1 mark for reference; 1 mark for comment (×2).

   Possible answers include:
   - Marie is angry "Marie doesn't turn"
   - Marie is shocked "Marie turns startled"
   - Marie loses control of her emotions "… laugh hysterically"
   - Marie is frightened "Marie backs off a step"
   - Marie loses her temper "Suddenly Marie flies at her"

3. Candidates should make some of the following possible observations:
   - she destroys Michael's photograph which is surprising as it has been a symbol of her adulation/has dominated the setting/staging
   - she is aggressive in destroying the photograph which is surprising because she is usually calm
   - she immediately tidies up which is surprising because she seems to accept this as "closure"/returns to domestic role

4. Candidates should identify one attitude towards Marie (for 1 mark).

    Candidates should select a relevant piece of dialogue (for 1 mark) and explain fully how this conveys the attitude (for 1 mark).

    Possible answers include:

    - **identification of attitude:** Deirdre is at points surprised/confused/upset/aggressive/calm/inquisitive
    - "But you'd know ..." seeks the truth
    - "here, that's you got everything back" implies resentment
    - "I want the truth out of you. I mean it." short sentences gives emphatic tone/impatience/assertiveness
    - "Tell me!" exclamation/monosyllabic words indicate(s) impatience
    - "Just the fella she's got living with her just now." indicates she is accepting/philosophical about being a victim of domestic violence

5. Candidates should identify areas of conflict in the characters' lives from this scene and elsewhere in the play.

    Possible areas for comment include:

    - Marie and Deirdre seem to resolve their conflict as an understanding is reached between them by the end of the play
    - Cassie and Nora's conflict grows as Cassie's plan to move away is revealed and she does not accept the truth about her father
    - there is ongoing political conflict in the world beyond the immediate setting of the play
    - there is conflict between the characters and their bleak setting. There are continued references to the blandness/drabness of the setting
    - conflict between men and women is a feature of the play. There are several examples of ongoing clashes between stereotypical male and female behaviour
    - there is conflict between Cassie and Marie over the issue of infidelity.
    - reference to the knife being a symbol of conflict

    Candidates may choose to answer in **bullet points** in this final question, or write a number of linked statements. There is **no requirement** to write a "mini essay".

    Up to 2 marks can be achieved for identifying elements of commonality as requested in the question. A further 2 marks can be achieved for **reference to the extract given.**

    4 additional marks can be awarded for similar references to **at least one other part of the text.**

    In practice this means:

    Identification of commonality (e.g. theme, central relationship, importance of setting, use of imagery, development in characterisation, use of personal experience, use of dramatic devices or any other key element ...)

    From the extract:

    1 relevant reference to technique; 1 appropriate comment

    OR 1 relevant reference to idea; 1 appropriate comment

    OR 1 relevant reference to feature; 1 appropriate comment

    OR 1 relevant reference to text; 1 appropriate comment

    (maximum of 2 marks only for discussion of extract)

    from **at least one other part of the text:**

    as above (×2) for **up to 4 marks**

PART A — DRAMA — *Sailmaker* by Alan Spence

6. Candidates should make four key points.

    Possible answers include:

    - Davie does not realise that Alec actually does need him/would like him to use his skills
    - Davie is already making excuses about not fixing up the yacht immediately
    - Davie indulges in unlawful gambling
    - Davie's lack of preparedness/homemaking skills
    - Does not provide financially for his family
    - asks Alec to go to the bookies for him against his will

7. For full marks candidates should identify two different aspects of Davie's mood, e.g. positive and negative, with supporting quotation/reference.

    Possible answers include:

    - **Lines 2–3:**

      Davie's mood is: sad, depressing, pessimistic, rejected, worthless, futile, angry, etc. (when discussing being made redundant as a sailmaker) "chucked"/"Nothin else doin"/"Nae work"/"Naebody needs sailmakers"

    - **Lines 10–16:**

      Davie's mood is optimistic, hopeful, humorous, excited, etc (when speaking about gambling) "wait an see"/"Who knows?"/"Maybe my coupon'll come up"/exaggerations about potential activity with winnings/"Never mind"/"Some ae these days"

8. (a) *Possible answers include:*

    - it is against the law to gamble
    - occasionally the bookmaker gets caught
    - gamblers protect their identity/avoid getting caught

    (b) Two clear points required for full marks (1 + 1).

    Possible answers include:

    - reveals he still considers himself a sailmaker pride/sense of identity/sense of importance

9. *Possible areas for comment include:*

    From the extract:

    - Alec gives Davie the yacht believing that he will fix it up represents his belief that Davie will live up to his promises
    - Davie speaks knowledgably about the yacht revealing his past as a skilled worker
    - Davie is already making excuses about why he can't fix up the yacht now

    From elsewhere:

    - Alec speaks with admiration about his father's past as a Sailmaker to Ian, and believes that his dad will fix up the yacht for him to play with

- Davie's continual lack of action in fixing the yacht represents his general procrastination in other matters/his bitterness at not being a Sailmaker/his prioritising (both in time and money) of gambling, drinking, etc.
- by contrast Billy paints the yacht immediately revealing that he is a different character who is proactive and keeps his word
- Alec places the yacht in the Glory Hole when his dad loses his job as he realises this is not a good time for his dad to be reminded of it
- Alec is accepting that his dad may not live up to his promises
- in the final scene of the play the yacht is placed on the fire by Alec and Davie which shows an acceptance from Alec about the type of person/ father that Davie is
- also represents the theme(s) of escape/childhood play, and relates to some of the music in the text, e.g. Red Sails in the Sunset, Will Your Anchor Hold, etc.

Candidates may choose to answer in **bullet points** in this final question, or write a number of linked statements. There is **no requirement** to write a "mini essay".

Up to 2 marks can be achieved for identifying elements of commonality as requested in the question. A further 2 marks can be achieved for **reference to the extract given.**

4 additional marks can be awarded for similar references to **at least one other part of the text.**

In practice this means:

Identification of commonality (e.g. theme, central relationship, importance of setting, use of imagery, development in characterisation, use of personal experience, use of dramatic devices or any other key element …)

from the extract:

1 relevant reference to technique; 1 appropriate comment

OR 1 relevant reference to idea; 1 appropriate comment

OR 1 relevant reference to feature; 1 appropriate comment

OR 1 relevant reference to text; 1 appropriate comment

(maximum of 2 marks only for discussion of extract)

from **at least one other part of the text:**

as above (×2) for **up to 4 marks**

PART A — DRAMA — *Tally's Blood* **by Ann Marie Di Mambro**

10. Candidates should make four key points for 1 mark each.

    Any four points.

    Possible answers include:

    - Bridget accuses Rosinella of making Lucia leave
    - Rosinella is confused about why Bridget is angry
    - Bridget accuses Rosinella of interfering in her relationship with Franco by making her feel that it wasn't genuine
    - Rosinella denies Bridget's accusations
    - Rosinella is annoyed that Bridget mentions Franco or their relationship
    - Rosinella expresses how upset she is that Lucia has left because of how much she loves her

- Rosinella admits that she is glad that Lucia and Hughie will not be together
- Rosinella wants to pretend this argument did not happen
- Bridget reveals that she was pregnant with Franco's child

11. Candidates should deal with both word choice and sentence structure – 2 marks are available for each.

    1 mark for reference; 1 mark for comment (×2).

    Possible answers include:

    Word choice:

    - "you made me" e.g. suggests she is resentful of Rosinella's interference
    - "nothing (to him)" e.g. sense of worthlessness
    - "just a wee" e.g. sense of insignificance
    - "Scottish tart" e.g. lacking in importance or virtue
    - "no a day goes past …" e.g. lasting impact/ inescapable aspect
    - "Franco loved me" e.g. simplistic but bold statement

    Sentence structure:

    - use of/repetition of (Rosinella's) question e.g. to suggest her outrage
    - repeated "you" e.g. creating an accusatory tone
    - use of dash e.g. to suggest that Rosinella treated Bridget like an afterthought
    - short clipped sentence e.g. to show she powerfully disagrees with Rosinella
    - repetition of "Franco loved me" e.g. to suggest emphatic nature of her belief

12. Candidates should identify two different attitudes with a supporting reference for each attitude.

    1 mark for reference; 1 mark for comment (×2).

    Possible answers include:

    - confused e.g. use of questions/repeating Bridget's words
    - defensive e.g. "What did I ever do to you?"
    - annoyed e.g. "Angry"
    - rude e.g. calls Bridget "lady"
    - contemptuous e.g. "Dismissive"
    - trivialising e.g. "What you going on about now?"
    - shocked e.g. "shakes her head"/"backs off in disbelief"

13. *Possible areas for comment include:*

    From the extract:

    - family willing to defend each other e.g. Bridget taking on Rosinella for Hughie
    - family looking out for each other e.g. Rosinella and Massimo looking after Lucia even though she is not their child
    - family interfering in romantic relationships e.g. Rosinella disapproving of Hughie and Lucia as well as Bridget and Franco

From elsewhere:

- conflict e.g. family arguments about children not doing as expected by their parents or family (Massimo opening his own shop/Franco joining the army)
- love/loyalty: characters looking after family members e.g. Rosinella and her father in law, Bridget and Hughie with their mother and siblings, Rosinella and Massimo with Lucia

Candidates may choose to answer in **bullet points** in this final question, or write a number of linked statements. There is **no requirement** to write a "mini essay".

Up to 2 marks can be achieved for identifying elements of commonality as requested in the question. A further 2 marks can be achieved for **reference to the extract given**.

4 additional marks can be awarded for similar references to **at least one other part of the text.**

In practice this means:

Identification of commonality (e.g. theme, central relationship, importance of setting, use of imagery, development in characterisation, use of personal experience, use of dramatic devices or any other key element …)

from the extract:

1 relevant reference to technique; 1 appropriate comment

OR 1 relevant reference to idea; 1 appropriate comment

OR 1 relevant reference to feature; 1 appropriate comment

OR 1 relevant reference to text; 1 appropriate comment

(maximum of 2 marks only for discussion of extract)

from **at least one other part of the text:**

as above (×2) for **up to 4 marks**

PART B – PROSE – *The Cone-Gatherers* **by Robin Jenkins**

14. Candidates should explain how the writer uses two examples of language to effectively describe Roderick's imaginings.

Reference should be made to lines 1–9.

1 mark for reference; 1 mark for comment (×2).

Possible answers include:

Word choice:

- "yew" has connotations of/links with death/Roderick imagines the cone-gatherers dead/murdered
- "stalking" describes Duror's walk as predatory
- "gloat" describes Duror's sense of smug satisfaction

Contrast:

- the reference to "tall"/"frowned" and "small"/ "smiled" to illustrate the differences in the two men

Sound:

- (onomatopoeia of) "cracked" suggests the loud/ clear/frightening sound of the gunfire

Imagery:

- "idea took root" links with trees and suggests the thought forming/developing in Roderick's mind
- "green bony arms" personifies the branches and suggests care/support

Sentence structure:

- short sentence "That idea sprouted" adds impact due to its brevity. Suggests the importance of Roderick's thoughts

15. Candidates should explain two different ways in which Roderick thinks of death in lines 10–19.

Candidates should use their own words as far as possible.

Possible answers include:

- "distant death was commonplace" – Roderick thinks of death as far away and/or a normal/regular occurrence
- "loyally been pleased" – Roderick thinks it is honourable/death of enemy is a good thing/he is patriotic
- "death … as a tyrant" – Roderick thought of death as cruel when it took someone he loved (his grandfather)/personally affected him
- imagines the death of Duror as a sense of despair/ damage/hopelessness …

16. Candidates should explain how the writer uses two examples of language to create a frightening atmosphere in lines 17–24.

1 mark for reference; 1 mark for comment (×2).

Possible answers include:

- reference to "desolation" suggests world completely barren
- reference to (every single leaf was) polluted suggests toxic atmosphere, etc.
- image of deaths gathering to seek revenge suggests that Roderick fears his earlier loyalty/patriotism was wrong
- question (about the death of evil and triumph of good) suggests that Roderick is unsure of the power of goodness
- atmosphere of darkness and silence, created by lack of sun and birdsong suggests an eerie quiet/the calm before the storm
- reference to the "hut in shadow" is typical of the horror genre/suggests evil to follow
- Roderick is too frightened to either cry or pray suggests he is overcome by the power of evil in the wood

17. 1 mark for reference; 1 mark for comment (×2).

Possible answers include:

- "Without any interpretable gesture" suggests his actions are hard to understand/confusing
- "without a sound" suggests stealth/sinister movements
- "(turned and) vanished" suggests sudden/magical disappearance
- "(as if this time) forever" suggests finality

18. Candidates should discuss why war is an important feature in this extract and elsewhere in the novel.

Possible areas for comment include:

- the setting of war is important as it places the characters in the wood at the same time: the brothers to gather cones, Duror to manage the estate and Lady Runcie-Campbell in charge in the absence of Sir Colin

- **OR** the war reflects the conflict within and between a number of characters – e.g. within Duror/between him and the cone-gatherers/Roderick and the class system ...

From the extract:

- Roderick is reminded of the war and its many deaths which he had initially greeted with patriotic loyalty
- **OR** the news of deaths heard on the radio is a regular feature and influences Roderick's thoughts of death in the woods, adding to his fears

From elsewhere:

- initial description of setting — idyllic with the subtle reference to the destroyer
- Duror is at war with himself — acknowledged on many occasions throughout the novel, often by references to sick/dying trees
- Duror's frustration at being too old to enlist partly fuels his hatred of the cone-gatherers
- Duror's wish to eliminate the cone-gatherers from the wood is linked to his sympathies for Hitler's actions against the Jews
- the war has allowed Duror to have the power that he has on the estate: Sir Colin is absent and Lady Runcie-Campbell relies on him for advice on estate management
- the wood is a microcosm of the world at war — Duror is waging his own war on the cone-gatherers whom he sees as inferior and should be eliminated; his own death at the end can be likened to Hitler's suicide

Candidates may choose to answer in **bullet points** in this final question, or write a number of linked statements. There is **no requirement** to write a "mini essay".

Up to 2 marks can be achieved for identifying elements of commonality as requested in the question. A further 2 marks can be achieved for **reference to the extract given.**

4 additional marks can be awarded for similar references to **at least one other part of the text.**

In practice this means:

Identification of commonality (e.g. theme, central relationship, importance of setting, use of imagery, development in characterisation, use of personal experience, use of dramatic devices or any other key element ...)

from the extract:

1 relevant reference to technique; 1 appropriate comment

OR 1 relevant reference to idea; 1 appropriate comment

OR 1 relevant reference to feature; 1 appropriate comment

OR 1 relevant reference to text; 1 appropriate comment

(maximum of 2 marks only for discussion of extract)

from **at least one other part of the text:**

as above (×2) for **up to 4 marks**

PART B – PROSE – *The Testament of Gideon Mack* by James Robertson

19. Four relevant points for 1 mark each.

    Candidates should use their own words as far as possible.

    Possible answers include:

    - Mack is discovered alive and with no serious injury his speedy recovery surprises doctors

- he doesn't seem keen to start back at his job
- he tells people about his ordeal and says he met the Devil who rescued him
- people think he has gone mad or similar and some are cross that he is saying things which are unchristian
- Mack takes the funeral of a friend but this is controversial as he speaks of meeting the Devil here too
- he is reported to the Presbytery
- there is a sort of a trial and Mack admits to what he has done but doesn't see anything wrong in it
- he is suspended until the main trial can take place but before that can happen Mack disappears

20. 1 mark for reference; 1 mark for comment (×2).

    Possible answers include:

    - "apparently" suggests it is not certain
    - "(even more) amazingly" **OR** reference to parenthesis suggests incredulity
    - "somehow" suggests near impossibility
    - "no creature ... survive" suggests he should not have lived through it
    - "astonished" suggests no-one can believe it

21. 1 mark for reference; 1 mark for comment (×2).

    Possible answers include:

    - "no great hurry ... duties" suggests lazy/distracted
    - "claimed"/"improbable"/"unorthodox"/reference to the unlikely story suggests madness or delusions
    - "assert"/"insisted" suggests he is convinced of it/ sure of himself/strength of character
    - "frailty" suggests weakness
    - "irreverent"/"scandalous"/"incompatible ... minister"/"no option but to refer" suggests he is offensive/blasphemous

22. *Possible areas for comment include:*

    - Candidates should identify one theme introduced in this extract and discuss how it is explored elsewhere in the novel.

    Possible themes include:

    - truth
    - religion
    - the supernatural
    - stories within stories
    - madness
    - belief

Candidates may choose to answer in **bullet points** in this final question, or write a number of linked statements. There is **no requirement** to write a "mini essay".

Up to 2 marks can be achieved for identifying elements of commonality as requested in the question. A further 2 marks can be achieved for **reference to the extract given.**

4 additional marks can be awarded for similar references to **at least one other part of the text.**

In practice this means:

Identification of commonality (e.g. theme, central relationship, importance of setting, use of imagery, development in characterisation, use of personal experience, use of dramatic devices or any other key element …)

from the extract:

1 relevant reference to technique; 1 appropriate comment

OR 1 relevant reference to idea; 1 appropriate comment

OR 1 relevant reference to feature; 1 appropriate comment

OR 1 relevant reference to text; 1 appropriate comment

(maximum of 2 marks only for discussion of extract)

from **at least one other part of the text:**

as above (×2) for **up to 4 marks**

PART B – PROSE – *Kidnapped* by Robert Louis Stevenson

23. 1 mark for reference; 1 mark for comment (×2).

    Possible answers include:

    - "it was so dark inside"/"in the pitch darkness" suggests going into the unknown
    - "a body could scarce breathe" holding breath due to fear
    - "with a beating heart" infers heart beating fast due to danger
    - "Minding my uncle's word about the banisters" infers thinking about warning (outlined by his uncle)
    - "I pushed out with foot and hand" proceeded carefully due to fear
    - "by the touch" indicates caution as he feels his way in the dark
    - "felt my way" indicates caution as he feels his way in the dark

24. 1 mark for realisation; 1 mark for mood.

    Possible answers include:

    Realisation:

    - Ebenezer has tried to kill David by sending him to the tower

    Mood:

    - David feels furious/David wishes to gain some revenge for his uncle's actions/David is determined to get revenge even if it causes him harm in the process/David feels some bravery at the realisation

25. *Possible answers include:*

    - David reaches the top of the stairs
    - David realises there is nothing there
    - he discovers that the staircase ends suddenly
    - he realises he is in great danger/he could have died
    - he is physically affected by fear
    - he starts to make his way down
    - his downward journey is full of anger
    - the storm rises
    - he sees a light in the kitchen
    - he sees his uncle
    - there is loud thunder

26. 1 mark for reference; 1 mark for comment.

    Possible answers include:

    - "wind sprang up" emphasises the suddenness and speed that the wind appears

- "clap" emphasises the physical power and suddenness of the wind
- "died (again)" emphasises the speed that the wind disappeared
- "it fell in buckets" the volume of rain is emphasised in that it seemed to be torrential
- "blinding flash" the intensity of the lightning is emphasised
- "tow-row" emphasises the very noisy nature of the thunder

27. *Possible areas for comment include:*

    - David's kidnapping
    - the roundhouse scene on the Covenant
    - the murder of Red Fox
    - the escape across the heather
    - the tension after the card game at Cluny's Cage
    - any of the many moments of tension between David and Alan throughout the novel
    - the confrontation with Ebenezer at the end of the novel

    Candidates may choose to answer in **bullet points** in this final question, or write a number of linked statements. There is **no requirement** to write a "mini essay".

    Up to 2 marks can be achieved for identifying elements of commonality as requested in the question. A further 2 marks can be achieved for **reference to the extract given**.

    4 additional marks can be awarded for similar references to **at least one other part of the text**.

    <u>In practice this means:</u>

    Identification of commonality (e.g. theme, central relationship, importance of setting, use of imagery, development in characterisation, use of personal experience, use of dramatic devices or any other key element …)

    from the extract:

    1 relevant reference to technique; 1 appropriate comment

    OR 1 relevant reference to idea; 1 appropriate comment

    OR 1 relevant reference to feature; 1 appropriate comment

    OR 1 relevant reference to text; 1 appropriate comment

    (maximum of 2 marks only for discussion of extract)

    from **at least one other part of the text:**

    as above (×2) for **up to 4 marks**

PART B – PROSE – *The Painter* by Iain Crichton Smith

28. 1 mark for reference; 1 mark for comment.

    Possible answers include:

    - "sitting comfortably"

      relaxed/at ease/calm

    - "no expression"

      impassive/detached/disengaged

    - "cold clear intensity"/reference to alliteration

      indifferent/focused/unresponsive

29. 1 mark for reference; 1 mark for comment (×2).

    Possible answers include:

    - "scythes" is a dangerous implement

- "swing" highlights dangerous nature of weapons/how they were being used
- "contorted" suggests intensity/strength of their anger distorts their faces
- "fury" suggests fierce/angry nature of the encounter
- "(of) battle" suggests a fierce/powerful/hostile encounter
- "suffused" suggests full of/consumed/visibly roused
- "blood" suggests violence/harm
- "(and) rage" suggests intense/deep-rooted/ passionate hatred for each other
- repetition of "as" conveys the energy/tension/ physical nature of the fight
- "teeth drawn … snarl" suggests animal-like brutality

30. *Possible answers include:*

"admiration"

- his ability to remain focused on his work
- the depth/single-mindedness of his focus
- his disregard for his own safety

"bitter disgust"

- his detachment/isolation from the villagers ("gaze … beyond the human")
- his impartial/unemotional stance
- his coldness/superiority to those around him (comparison to hawk)
- his reaction to the disruption to his painting ("blind fury")
- his visible emotion relating to the conflict ("tears of rage"/"still snarling")
- his departure from the conflict with the narrator

31. *Possible answers include:*

- he is ignored
- they are troubled by him/they don't understand him
- he is seen as being different/an outsider
- he is rejected
- his work is destroyed
- he does not conform with their code of conduct

32. *Possible areas for comment include:*

- **"The Telegram"** — the "thin woman's" reputation as an outsider due to the sacrifices she has made for her son
- **"The Red Door"** — Murdo's discontent leading to his desire to be independent from the constraints of village life; Mary's independence shown by her choice of clothing/creativity, etc.
- **"Mother and Son"** — John's isolation from his peers/ lack of confidence due to his mother's constant criticism/control/dominance
- **"In Church"** — "The priest" (a deserter who is in hiding) is at odds with society, having lost all sense of humanity
- **"The Crater"** — Robert feels at odds with his role as an Officer in a war time situation

Candidates may choose to answer in **bullet points** in this final question, or write a number of linked statements. There is **no requirement** to write a "mini essay".

Up to 2 marks can be achieved for identifying elements of commonality as requested in the question. A further 2 marks can be achieved for **reference to the extract given**.

4 additional marks can be awarded for similar references to **at least one other part of the text**.

In practice this means:

Identification of commonality (e.g. theme, central relationship, importance of setting, use of imagery, development in characterisation, use of personal experience, use of dramatic devices or any other key element …)

from the extract:

1 relevant reference to technique; 1 appropriate comment

OR 1 relevant reference to idea; 1 appropriate comment

OR 1 relevant reference to feature; 1 appropriate comment

OR 1 relevant reference to text; 1 appropriate comment

(maximum of 2 marks only for discussion of extract)

from **at least one other part of the text**:

as above (×2) for **up to 4 marks**

PART B — PROSE — *Dear Santa* **by Anne Donovan**

33. Four points for 1 mark each.

Possible answers include:

- Alison is writing a letter to Santa
- she is trying to ask him to make her mother love her
- she is finding writing the letter difficult
- she doesn't believe Santa can make her mother love her
- she isn't sure if she believes in Santa
- she is feeling unhappy/pessimistic
- her mother comes into the bedroom/looks after Katie/spends time with Alison
- Alison finishes the letter but does not ask for what she really wants
- Alison and her mother spend some close/loving time together
- Alison demonstrates her affection for her mother
- Alison's mother demonstrates a little affection towards Alison
- at the end of the extract it is suggested there is hope for their relationship

34. 1 mark for reference; 1 mark for comment.

Possible answers include:

- "the page ah'm starin at" suggests it is hard for her to start the letter
- "it's hard tae find the words" shows she finds it difficult to say what she really wants/feels
- unfinished sentences emphasise how hard she finds it to put her feelings into words
- repeated questions suggest she doubts her request would work
- negative answers reinforce the fact that she doubts whether a letter to Santa would be effective
- reference to grey outside/no white Christmas reflects the negativity of her mood
- the fact that she doesn't write down what she actually wants shows she doesn't think it's achievable

35. (a) 1 mark for reference; 1 mark for comment.

Possible answers include:

- "Hair glowin like a halo" — suggests angelic, connotations of goodness, bringing light into darkness, positivity, etc.
- (hair) "soft and fuzzy" — makes the mother seem kind and gentle
- "she's in a good mood", etc. suggests she's mellowed towards Alison and is allowing her to be closer
- "There's nothing wrang wi broon hair" suggests she understands Alison wants to be more like her and Katie but she reassures her that she is fine the way she is
- "She looks at me mair soft like" — suggests more loving
- "She kisses me" — suggests affection
- "nearly", or reference to "a wee crack of light" suggests hope that the relationship can be rebuilt/ that there is some love there

(b) 1 mark for reference; 1 mark for comment.

Possible answers showing negative contrast include:

- "she cannae be bothered wi that"/"jerks her heid away"/"sayin don't"/"you'll mess it up" suggests mother doesn't like physical contact with Alison
- "dry (kiss)" suggests limited, grudging, etc.
- "barely grazing" suggests mother hasn't much time for Alison
- "before ah've kissed her back" suggests she does not really want physical contact with Alison
- "closin the door" suggests putting up a barrier between herself and Alison, or similar

36. *Possible areas for comment include:*

- **"Virtual Pals"** — Siobhan's lack of confidence; boyfriend issues; growing up; relationships
- **"Zimmerobics"** — old age and associated problems; loneliness
- **"All that Glisters"** — how Clare copes with her father's illness and death; how she copes with difficult adults such as the shopkeeper and her aunt; how she overcomes challenges; how she supports her mother in her grief; how she celebrates her daddy
- **"A Chitterin Bite"** — relationships; lack of confidence; inability to move on; as a child, Mary does not deal well with Agnes growing up and moving on; as an adult, she resolves her personal difficulties by taking control and ending the affair

Candidates may choose to answer in **bullet points** in this final question, or write a number of linked statements. There is **no requirement** to write a "mini essay".

Up to 2 marks can be achieved for identifying elements of commonality as requested in the question. A further 2 marks can be achieved for **reference to the extract given.**

4 additional marks can be awarded for similar references to **at least one other part of the text.**

<u>In practice this means:</u>

Identification of commonality (e.g. theme, central relationship, importance of setting, use of imagery, development in characterisation, use of personal experience, use of dramatic devices or any other key element ...)

from the extract:

1 relevant reference to technique; 1 appropriate comment

OR 1 relevant reference to idea; 1 appropriate comment

OR 1 relevant reference to feature; 1 appropriate comment

OR 1 relevant reference to text; 1 appropriate comment

(maximum of 2 marks only for discussion of extract)

from **at least one other part of the text:**

as above (×2) for **up to 4 marks**

PART C — POETRY — *Originally* by Carol Ann Duffy

37. 1 mark for each point made. Candidates must use their own words.

Possible answers include:

- gloss of "red room" — reference to vehicle
- gloss of "fell" — travelled downhill/in a downwards direction
- gloss of "through the fields" — travelled through the country/countryside
- gloss of "mother singing" — reference to her mother's voice
- gloss of "My brothers cried"/"bawling" — brothers being upset
- gloss of "miles rushed back ... etc." — sense of leaving somewhere/distance
- gloss of "toy ... holding its paw, etc." — had comfort of toy/teddy

38. 1 mark for reference; 1 mark for comment (×2).

Possible answers include:

- "slow" a gradual awareness of the new surroundings/a gradual build-up of feelings in response to the move
- "leaving you standing" you find yourself isolated
- "resigned" you have to accept things/learn to accept things
- "up an avenue" you can be lonely
- "sudden" change can seem quick/unexpected
- "Your accent wrong" you feel out of place/don't fit in
- "unimagined" you haven't been able to picture new surroundings
- "pebble-dashed estates" find yourself in unfamiliar surroundings
- "big boys eating worms" people seem very different
- "shouting words you don't understand" language barriers
- "parents' anxiety" you sense other people's worries
- "stirred like a loose tooth" you become aware that things are different
- "I want our own country" you miss your old surroundings/want to return

39. 1 mark for reference; 1 mark for comment (×2).

Possible answers include:

- "But" suggests a change from being an outsider to accepting her new surroundings

- "then you forget/don't recall" suggests your memory blots out old life
- "change" you adapt to your surroundings
- "brother swallow a slug" suggests awareness that other family members are accepting the local culture
- "skelf of shame" suggests how little guilt is felt in accepting the local culture
- "my tongue … snake" suggests a casting off of old life, just as a snake casts off its old skin
- "my voice … like the rest" suggests she's fitting in with the local culture

40. 1 mark for reference; 1 mark for comment.

Possible answers include:

- the use of the title "Originally" rounds off/brings a sense of closure
- the use of "Originally" links back to the discussion of where you come from/your origins (an important theme of the poem)
- "hesitates" suggests uncertainty about national/cultural identity (one of the main themes of the poem)/suggests acceptance of new surroundings

41. *Possible areas for comment include:*

- **"Originally"** – memory, identity/sense of belonging/acceptance/isolation, etc.
- **"War Photographer"** – memory, painful memories, human cruelty, etc.
- **"Valentine"** – different aspects of love, relationships, etc.
- **"Havisham"** – jealousy/hard heartedness, rejection, etc.
- **"Anne Hathaway"** – love, relationships, etc.
- **"Mrs Midas"** – love, relationships, change, etc.

Other answers are possible.

Candidates may choose to answer in **bullet points** in this final question, or write a number of linked statements. There is **no requirement** to write a "mini essay".

Up to 2 marks can be achieved for identifying elements of commonality as requested in the question. A further 2 marks can be achieved for **reference to the extract given**.

4 additional marks can be awarded for similar references to **at least one other part of the text**.

In practice this means:

Identification of commonality (e.g. theme, central relationship, importance of setting, use of imagery, development in characterisation, use of personal experience, use of dramatic devices or any other key element …)

from the extract:

1 relevant reference to technique; 1 appropriate comment

OR 1 relevant reference to idea; 1 appropriate comment

OR 1 relevant reference to feature; 1 appropriate comment

OR 1 relevant reference to text; 1 appropriate comment

(**maximum of 2 marks only for discussion of extract**)

from **at least one other part of the text:**

as above (×2) for **up to 4 marks**

PART C – POETRY – *Good Friday* **by Edwin Morgan**

42. Two references plus comments on what we learn about the drunken man.

1 mark for reference; 1 mark for comment (×2).

Possible answers include:

- "D's this go"/"right along Bath Street?" shows that he's confused
- "I've got to get some Easter eggs for the kiddies" shows he is kind/generous
- "I don't say it's right" **OR** "I'm no saying it's right" shows he is aware that his drinking on a religious holiday could be disagreed with
- "ye understand – ye understand?" shows that he wants the poet to empathise/doesn't want to be judged harshly
- "I'm no boring you, eh?" shows his desire to be listened to/accepted

43. (a) 1 mark for reference; 1 mark for comment.

Possible answers include:

- use of Glaswegian dialect suggests sense of place
- use of second person suggests the man is speaking directly to someone else
- use of long winding sentences suggests the man is rambling
- use of dashes/pauses suggests hesitation/loss of train of thought
- use of questions suggests he's seeking agreement
- use of repetition suggests immediacy of speech

(b) 1 mark for reference; 1 mark for identification of idea or concern (×2).

Possible answers include:

- "take today, I don't know what today's in aid of" suggests e.g. (religious) ignorance
- "whether Christ was – crucified or was he–" suggests e.g. religious doubt/ignorance
- "You're an educatit man, you can tell me" suggests e.g. awareness of class/educational differences
- "the working man has nae education" suggests e.g. awareness of lack of opportunities
- "he's just bliddy ignorant" suggests e.g. awareness/acceptance of lack of education

44. For 2 marks, candidates should refer to a feature of the last five lines and how it effectively continues an idea/language feature from earlier in the poem.

Possible answers include:

- "The bus brakes violently" echoes the opening lines which focus on the bus's movements
- "He lunges for the stair, swings down – off" echoes the opening lines which focus on the drunken man's movements
- "for his Easter eggs" recalls the drunk man's task/setting in time/title
- the structure of the last few lines

OR

> "on very
>> nearly
>>> steady
>>>> legs"

emphasises the man's drunkenness

45. *Possible comments on other poems:*

- **"Good Friday"** — religion, compassion, class in terms of education

- **"Trio"** — supernatural, passing of time, alienation, religion

- **"Slate"** — change, i.e. making a fresh start (politically or personally), change over time, adapting to change, identity, hopeful

- **"Hyena"** — death, brutality, survival, isolation, fear, perseverance of the hunter, alienation through fear, suffering

- **"In the Snack Bar"** — determination, compassion, isolation, perseverance, alienation, helplessness, suffering

- **"Winter"** — death and the relentless passing of time, progress of time, aging, suffering

Candidates may choose to answer in **bullet points** in this final question, or write a number of linked statements. There is **no requirement** to write a "mini essay".

Up to 2 marks can be achieved for identifying elements of commonality as requested in the question. A further 2 marks can be achieved for **reference to the extract given.**

4 additional marks can be awarded for similar references to **at least one other part of the text.**

<u>In practice this means:</u>

Identification of commonality (e.g. theme, central relationship, importance of setting, use of imagery, development in characterisation, use of personal experience, use of dramatic devices or any other key element ...)

from the extract:

1 relevant reference to technique; 1 appropriate comment

OR 1 relevant reference to idea; 1 appropriate comment

OR 1 relevant reference to feature; 1 appropriate comment

OR 1 relevant reference to text; 1 appropriate comment

(maximum of 2 marks only for discussion of extract)

from **at least one other part of the text:**

as above (×2) for **up to 4 marks**

PART C — POETRY — *Sounds of the Day* by Norman MacCaig

46. Two points for 2 marks.

Possible answers include:

- he seems unconcerned/untroubled by them
- he seems comforted by them
- he reacts to them in a positive way
- they are familiar to him

47. 1 mark for reference; 1 mark for comment.

Possible answers include:

- "clatter" is a harsh/unsettling sound

- "creak" is an eerie sound/suggestive of the "door scraped shut" (which is to follow in line 10)

- "snuffling" suggests crying

- "puff" suggests something sudden

- "seeing us off" suggests aggression/parting

- "blocking ... unblocking" lack of constancy/ever changing

- "black drums rolled" suggests portent/sign of trouble

- "falling" suggests doom/troubling consequences

48. 1 mark for reference; 1 mark for comment (×2).

Possible answers include:

- "(door) scraped (shut)" harsh sound/contrasting sound with earlier (relative) calm

- "shut" is final/ominous

- "(the) end" suggests closed off/cut off/finality

- "all the sounds" suggests an all-encompassing change

- "you (left me)" contrast with "us" from verse 1/ sense of separation

- "left me" suggests isolation/loneliness/upset

- "quietest fire" suggests silence/is opposite of earlier normal sounds/oxymoron/paradox/superlative

49. 1 mark for reference; 1 mark for comment (×2).

Possible answers include:

- "I thought" suggests poet's uncertainty

- "hurt in my pride only" suggests initial limited impact

- "forgetting that" suggests impact was not immediate

- "plunge" impact was deep

- "freezing (water)" suggests cold/unpleasant effects

- "ice" suggests extreme coldness of feeling

- identification of image of "bangle of ice" image suggests memories/burden of memory/weight of memory

- "whole" suggests completeness of effect

- "numb" suggests he has been overwhelmed, etc.

50. *Possible areas for comment include:*

- **"Assisi"** — feelings of anger, outrage, bitterness

- **"Aunt Julia"** — feelings of nostalgia, loss, confusion, etc.

- **"Basking Shark"** — feelings of confusion, doubt, shock, etc.

- **"Visiting Hour"** — feelings of sadness, loss, unworthiness, etc.

- **"Memorial"** — sadness, loss, etc.

Candidates may choose to answer in **bullet points** in this final question, or write a number of linked statements. There is **no requirement** to write a "mini essay".

Up to 2 marks can be achieved for identifying elements of commonality as requested in the question. A further 2 marks can be achieved for **reference to the extract given.**

4 additional marks can be awarded for similar references to **at least one other part of the text.**

<u>In practice this means:</u>

Identification of commonality (e.g. theme, central relationship, importance of setting, use of imagery, development in characterisation, use of personal experience, use of dramatic devices or any other key element ...)

from the extract:

1 relevant reference to technique; 1 appropriate comment

OR 1 relevant reference to idea; 1 appropriate comment

OR 1 relevant reference to feature; 1 appropriate comment

OR 1 relevant reference to text; 1 appropriate comment

(maximum of 2 marks only for discussion of extract)

from **at least one other part of the text:**

as above (×2) for **up to 4 marks**

PART C — POETRY — *Keeping Orchids* by Jackie Kay

51. Candidates must use their own words as far as possible.

    1 mark for a valid answer (×2).

    Possible answers include:

    - the (first person) narrator describes what happens when she meets her mother for the first time

    - there is an awkward atmosphere between the two women

    - the mother gives the narrator flowers (orchids)

    - orchids are rare/exotic and (therefore) difficult to look after/this symbolises the precarious nature of their relationship

    - the vase of flowers spills twice /symbolises the fragile nature of their relationship

    - the narrator tries to sort out the flower arrangement but she is not good at it/symbolises her feelings of awkwardness

    - some of the buds stay shut

    - the narrator sees the flowers as a burden/responsibility (not a pleasure)

52. **Word choice:** 1 mark for reference; 1 mark for comment.

    Structure: 1 mark for reference; 1 mark for comment.

    Possible answers of word choice include:

    - "first (met)" establishes the importance of that moment

    - "twelve days later" shows how much time has elapsed since the meeting

    - "Twice since" shows the effort put in to take the flowers home

    - "Even after that" shows that time seems to be against the flowers

    - repetition of "twelve days later" reiterates the distance since the meeting time

    - "fading fast" suggests the haziness of time passing

    Possible answers on structure include:

    - the poem is written in couplets which gives a regular (predictable) pace/rhythm to indicate time passing steadily

    - there is repeated use of enjambment to indicate the pace of events

    - the frequent use of conjunctives moves the story of the poem forward at a fast pace

    - parenthesis is limited indicating the urgency to recount only the basic account of what happened

    - short sentences indicate the poet's intention to summarise events as succinctly as possible

    - repetition of "twice since" reiterates frequency of an event

53. 1 mark for reference; 1 mark for comment (×3).

    Possible answers include:

    - "voice rushes through a tunnel the other way" suggests distance

    - "try to remember" shows lack of clarity/shows the physical distance

    - "a paisley pattern scarf, a brooch" suggests the mother is dressed up for the occasion

    - "her hands, awkward and hard to hold" suggests lack of familiarity of touch

    - "fold and unfold" suggests the mother is fidgeting

    - "the story of her life" suggests lack of familiarity

    - "Compressed" suggests stiffness/only revealing the bare minimum of details

    - "Airtight" suggests defensiveness/being impenetrable

54. *Possible areas for comment include:*

    - the difference between appearance and reality

    - the conflict within family relationships

    - the difficulties of parenthood

    - the changing roles we perform as family members

    - the influence of time in shaping our memories/point of view

    - the importance of setting in shaping our behaviour/influencing our thinking

    - the complex nature of love

    - the acceptance of imperfection

    - the development of self-awareness through time

    - the complexities of degeneration/decay

    Candidates may choose to answer in **bullet points** in this final question, or write a number of linked statements. There is **no requirement** to write a "mini essay".

    Up to 2 marks can be achieved for identifying elements of commonality as requested in the question. A further 2 marks can be achieved for **reference to the extract given.**

    4 additional marks can be awarded for similar references to **at least one other part of the text.**

    In practice this means:

    Identification of commonality (e.g. theme, central relationship, importance of setting, use of imagery, development in characterisation, use of personal experience, use of dramatic devices or any other key element …)

    from the extract:

    1 relevant reference to technique; 1 appropriate comment

    OR 1 relevant reference to idea; 1 appropriate comment

    OR 1 relevant reference to feature; 1 appropriate comment

    OR 1 relevant reference to text; 1 appropriate comment

    (maximum of 2 marks only for discussion of extract)

    from **at least one other part of the text:**

    as above (×2) for **up to 4 marks**

SECTION 2 – Critical Essay

Bands are not grades. The five bands are designed primarily to assist with placing each candidate response at an appropriate point on a continuum of achievement. Assumptions about final grades or association of final grades with particular bands should not be allowed to influence objective assessment.

	20–18	17–14	13–10	9–5	4–0
The candidate demonstrates:	• **a high degree of familiarity** with the text as a whole • **very good understanding** of the central concerns of the text • a line of thought that is **consistently relevant to the task**	• **familiarity** with the text as a whole • **good understanding** of the central concerns of the text • a line of thought that is **relevant** to the task	• **some familiarity** with the text as a whole • **some understanding** of the central concerns of the text • a line of thought that is **mostly relevant** to the task	• **familiarity with some aspects** of the text • **attempts** a line of thought **but this may lack relevance to the task**	Although such essays should be rare, in this category, the candidate's essay will demonstrate one or more of the following • it contains numerous errors in spelling/grammar/punctuation/sentence construction/paragraphing • knowledge and understanding of the text(s) are not used to answer the question • any analysis and evaluation attempted are unconvincing • the answer is simply too thin
Analysis of the text demonstrates:	• **thorough awareness** of the writer's techniques, through analysis, making **confident** use of critical terminology • **very detailed/thoughtful** explanation of stylistic devices supported by a **range of well-chosen** references and/or quotations	• **sound awareness** of the writer's techniques through analysis, making **good** use of critical terminology • **detailed explanation** of stylistic devices supported by **appropriate** references and/or quotation	• **an awareness** of the writer's techniques through analysis, making **some use** of critical terminology • explanation of stylistic devices supported by **some appropriate** references and/or quotation	• **some awareness of the more obvious** techniques used by the writer • **description of some** stylistic devices followed by limited reference and/or quotation	
Evaluation of the text is shown through:	• **a well developed** commentary of what has been enjoyed/gained from the text(s), supported by a **range of well-chosen** references to its relevant features	• **a reasonably developed** commentary of what has been enjoyed/gained from the text (s), supported by **appropriate** references to its relevant features	• **some commentary** of what has been enjoyed/gained from the text(s), supported by **some appropriate** references to its relevant features	• **brief** commentary of what has been enjoyed/gained from the text(s), followed by **brief** reference to its features	
The candidate:	• uses language to communicate a line of thought **very clearly** • uses spelling, grammar, sentence construction and punctuation which are **consistently** accurate • structures the essay **effectively to enhance** meaning/purpose • uses paragraphing which is **accurate and effective**	• uses language to communicate a line of thought **clearly** • uses spelling, grammar, sentence construction and punctuation which are **mainly** accurate • structures the essay **well** • uses paragraphing which is **accurate**	• uses language to communicate a line of thought **at first reading** • uses spelling, grammar, sentence construction and punctuation which are **sufficiently** accurate • attempts to structure the essay **in an appropriate way** • uses paragraphing which is sufficiently accurate	• uses language to communicate a line of thought which may be disorganised and/or difficult to follow • makes significant errors in spelling/grammar/sentence construction/punctuation • has not structured the essay well • has made significant errors in paragraphing	
In summary, the candidates essay is:	thorough and precise	very detailed and shows some insight	fairly detailed and relevant	lacks detail and relevance	superficial and/or technically weak

NATIONAL 5 ENGLISH 2017

READING FOR UNDERSTANDING, ANALYSIS AND EVALUATION

1. 1 mark for any one reference; 1 mark for comment.

   Possible answers include:

   - "We played … every afternoon" suggests e.g. that it was their major pastime
   - "Sometimes other kids would join us" suggests e.g. occasionally they had more friends/bigger game/ community
   - "in the summer we never seemed to leave"/"game after game"/"sometimes until it got dark" suggests e.g. that they played constantly/all day
   - "endlessly" suggests e.g. enjoyment seemed never to stop
   - "absorbing" suggests e.g. that they found it fascinating/fulfilling/all-consuming
   - "dim glow of street lights" suggests e.g. nostalgia
   - "two litre bottle of orange squash" suggests e.g. simple childhood pleasures/nostalgia
   - "pass it from player to player" suggests e.g. camaraderie/innocence
   - "none of us deterred by [warmth]" suggests e.g. nothing would put them off
   - "it tasted good" suggests e.g. that the experience was pleasurable
     NB "good" on its own not sufficient.

2. Any four points.

   Glosses of:

   - "never made it onto the school team" e.g. was never picked/selected
     NB "team" need not be glossed.
   - "He kept trying"/"kept going to the trials"/"both at primary and senior school" e.g. persevered with opportunities for selection
   - "he was just off the pace" e.g. he was not quite fast/skilled enough
   - "He yearned to play" e.g. he longed to be part of/ play for the team
     NB Candidate must make reference to being in the team.
   - "He yearned … to progress" e.g. he longed to improve
   - "He yearned to… read out… (one of the honours of making the team)" e.g. he longed for his moment of glory

     *NB Candidate must refer to the intensity of the desire at least once if dealing with any of the **final three bullet points** (above).*

3. Any six points.

   Glosses of:

   - "98 per cent fail to make the transition (into professional football)"/"only a fraction made it (into professional football)" e.g. very few succeed
   - "Of those who made it into the district team, only a handful were picked by Reading, the local club"/"Perhaps none made it all the way to the top flight" e.g. even those who have some success didn't make it all the way/some progress doesn't necessarily mean success
   - "Many struggle to cope with rejection" e.g. many find it hard to come to terms with not being accepted
   - "many suffer anxiety" e.g. they are affected by stress
   - "many suffer …a loss of confidence" e.g. self-esteem/self-belief is undermined
   - "and, in some cases, depression" e.g. more serious mental health issues may develop
   - "These youngsters are often described as being "left on football's scrapheap" e.g. (inference) the process is heartless/rigorous/unfeeling
   - "it seems to me, though, that the number rejected is, in fact, far higher" e.g. those not selected exceeds number reported
   - "the sifting process starts from the first time you kick a ball at the local park" e.g. selection begins very early/there are many stages of filtering/selection
   - "the standard was high" e.g. the ability requirement is considerable
   - "I remember my heart beating out of my chest when the 'scouts' arrived" e.g. situation causes nerves/ pressure
   - "I was crushed by the disappointment" e.g. the distress (at failure) is overwhelming
   - "the race" e.g. the process is highly competitive
   - "… had only just started" e.g. the process is lengthy

4. - "Just as … so" structure may, but need not, be employed (1+1) e.g. just as there are many grains of sand on the beach so there are many people who don't succeed/are trying to succeed

   OR

   - any two areas of similarity. Ideas in common include multiplicity/identical or similar quality/anonymity/ insignificance/expendability/idea of being influenced by another/external/powerful force

5. 1 mark for any one reference; 1 mark for comment (×2).

   Possible answers include:

   Word choice:

   - "inevitable" makes clear the unavoidability of failure
   - "natural selection" or "evolution" makes clear e.g. survival of the fittest/that this is a process that has always existed
   - "part and parcel" — makes clear the essential nature/necessity of the process of selection

   Imagery:

   - "first lap"/"final straight"/reference to image of "race" — makes clear notion of a race/different stages of the process

     NB Do not reward a comment on "race" if the same word has been used as a reference.

   Sentence structure:

   - "But this is football."/"This is life."/short sentence(s) makes clear e.g. the fundamental/ inarguable truth

- repetition of "this is" makes clear e.g. that this is a statement of fact/inescapable
- repetition of "failure is…" makes clear e.g. the fact that success is not universal
- "Without losers, there cannot be winners."/"Without pain, there cannot be joy."/"Without natural selection, there cannot be evolution."/reference to balance/contrast of opposites makes clear e.g. that life has ups and downs
- "Without losers, there cannot be winners. Without pain, there cannot be joy. Without natural selection, there cannot be evolution."/similarity/antithetical construction (within or in consecutive sentence(s))/parallel structure makes clear e.g. that life has ups and downs
- "Failure is not the opposite of progress; failure is part and parcel of progress."/use of semi-colon makes clear e.g. failure is crucial to moving on

NB If no reference given, any comment cannot be rewarded.

NB For full marks two different language features must be dealt with.

6. Any three points.

Possible answers include:

- "The skills are transparent" the criteria for success are obvious
- "the opportunities exist" gives idea of chances being widely available
- "There is no room for family favours" gives idea of lack of nepotism
- "or cosy alliances" gives idea of lack of favourable treatment
- "The best of the best shine through" gives idea of the most talented individuals do make it
- "whether they are from a tough part of Liverpool, like Wayne Rooney, or raised in grinding poverty in Uruguay, like Luis Suárez" gives idea of irrelevance of background

7. Any five points.

Glosses of:

- "Youngsters who are educated and self-assured are likely to be better footballers, too" e.g. young people who have done well at school AND who are confident will perform more effectively
- "The Ancient Greeks understood this only too well" e.g. it has been known for a long time
- "(the humane idea) that the mind and body grow together" e.g. that emotional and physical development go hand in hand
- "The German football system has embraced this truth, too" e.g. this is recognised abroad
- "Such a cultural transformation needs to happen here, too" e.g. the lessons learned abroad should be considered in Britain
- "It is that we need to redefine our relationship with failure" e.g. we must reappraise how we view failure
- "not just in football but in life" e.g. we need to rethink how we deal with failure in areas other than football

- "losing is an essential (indeed, a beautiful) part of life" e.g. experiencing failure is necessary/natural
- "beautiful" e.g. failure can be viewed positively
- "the empowering idea that failure is less important, infinitely less so, than how we respond to it" e.g. how we react to failure is crucial/gives us strength/inspiration
- "Failing (to make the grade at football) is crushing" e.g. not being accepted (as a footballer) is devastating
- "It is natural to be sad" e.g. misery is to be expected/part of what we are
- "But it is also a pathway to a new reality" e.g. but leads us to a different life

NB Candidates may use the word 'failure' in their response without penalty.

8. 1 mark for any one reference; 1 mark for comment.

Possible answers include:

- similarity of sentence openings/rule of three construction/"Tens of thousands … Hundreds of thousands … Tens of millions" highlights idea of scale/size of competition
- "But" highlights the shift towards the positive side to failure
- short sentence/"But this is not the end of life."/"It is merely the beginning." highlights that all is not lost
- repetition of "a new"/rule of three construction/climactic structure/"a new dream, a new hope, a new way of finding meaning" highlights the possibility of a fresh start

NB Do not accept list.

9. 1 mark for any one selection from lines 60–64; 1 mark for linked reference or explanation from elsewhere.

Possible answers include:

- reference to Mark/relates to earlier mentions of Mark
- use of first person/relates to earlier use of first person
- "failures (in football)" revisits important idea expressed by e.g. "never made it onto the school team", etc.
- "so important, so trivial"/"Life is too short, too precious, to be derailed by failure" revisits important idea expressed by e.g. "failing to make the grade at football is crushing … but it is also the pathway to a new reality"

NB Answer may address the idea of importance or triviality.

- "never deterred him" revisits important idea expressed by e.g. "He kept trying"
- "new dreams"/"new aspirations" repeats earlier use of word/idea
- "accept" repeats earlier use of word/idea
- "embrace" repeats earlier use of word/idea
- reference to a linguistic element from the final paragraph, e.g. repetition of word "too"/"we have"/sentence structure/short sentences/short paragraph(s) suggests emphatic nature of final summing up comments

NB Do not reward a response that simply says 'it sums up the main ideas of the passage, etc.' unless the candidate goes on to explain what the main idea is.

CRITICAL READING

SECTION 1 – SCOTTISH TEXT

PART A – DRAMA – *Bold Girls* **by Rona Munro**

1. Any four points for 1 mark each.

    Candidates should use their own words.

    Possible answers include:

    - the women's lives can be disrupted by authoritative raids
    - they accept raids as part of life
    - the women's lives are mundane and a 'simple' night out can be looked forward to
    - the women speak frankly to each other
    - the women know their life style is not healthy
    - the omen are supportive of each other
    - Marie, Cassie and Nora are suspicious of Deirdre
    - there is tension between Cassie and Deirdre
    - Nora uses domesticity to comfort herself from the harshness of reality

2. 1 mark for reference; 1 mark for comment.

    Possible examples of humour include:

    - "It's the D.Ts" suggests irreverence/laughing at herself
    - "… the film stars have"/"Me and Joan Collins both" suggests exaggeration/mock self-importance
    - "… all the excitement" suggests sarcasm
    - "… would your manicure stand up to the closest inspection" suggests irony

3. (a) 1 mark for reference; 1 mark for comment.

    Possible answers include:

    - "Let's see Marie's hand there." suggests good humour between them
    - "Ah she's got a clear conscience." indicates respect for Marie
    - "Wired up but not plugged in." suggests humour/banter

    (b) 1 mark for reference; 1 mark for comment.

    Possible answers include:

    - "black wee heart"/"thieve the clothes"/"nail the wee snake down"/"… if it is Deirdre?" shows Cassie distrusts Deirdre
    - "It is." shows Deirdre stands up to Cassie
    - "I hope you've not taken a fancy … your eye" shows lack of trust

4. 1 mark for reference; 1 mark for comment.

    Possible answers include:

    - "What?" shows confrontation/confusion/defensiveness
    - "That I saw you before." shows accusation/confrontation
    - "you're a lying hoor …" shows the anger/hostility Cassie feels towards Deirdre
    - "… you never saw anything." shows defiance/threat/denial
    - any part of "With a man. With him. With – " suggests build up to revelation

    - identification of ellipsis suggests anticipation
    - any reference to "Cassie lunges at her before she can get another word out" suggests desperation to stop her/aggression

5. Candidates are likely to include many different aspects of the mother–daughter theme.

    Possible areas for comment include:

    - despite Nora and Cassie's "bickering" they constantly support each other (especially with domestic hardships/challenges)
    - Hostilities due to memories of past relationship with father
    - Marie and Deirdre are likely to form a "mother/daughter" relationship despite the fact they are not directly blood relatives
    - Nora and Cassie "mother" Marie as they see her as a lone parent left in difficult circumstances (i.e. widowed and alone)
    - Deirdre and her biological mother are not close (as demonstrated by the fact that Deirdre is the victim of domestic violence perpetrated by her mother's latest boyfriend)

    Candidates may choose to answer in **bullet points** in this final question, or write a number of linked statements. There is **no requirement** to write a "mini essay".

    Up to 2 marks can be achieved for identifying elements of commonality as requested in the question. A further 2 marks can be achieved for **reference to the extract given**.

    4 additional marks can be awarded for similar references to **at least one other part of the text**.

    <u>In practice this means:</u>

    Identification of commonality (e.g. theme, central relationship, importance of setting, use of imagery, development in characterisation, use of personal experience, use of narrative style or any other key element …)

    From the extract:

    1 relevant reference to technique; 1 appropriate comment

    OR 1 relevant reference to idea; 1 appropriate comment

    OR 1 relevant reference to feature; 1 appropriate comment

    OR 1 relevant reference to text; 1 appropriate comment

    (maximum of 2 marks only for discussion of extract)

    from at **least one other part of the text:**

    as above (×2) for **up to 4 marks.**

PART A – DRAMA – *Sailmaker* **by Alan Spence**

6. 1 mark for identifying an aspect of Alec's attitude; 1 mark for supporting reference (×2).

    Possible answers include:

    - Alec is trying to understand his father e.g. by asking about his dad's reasons for gambling
    - Alec has some admiration for his dad in the past e.g. memories of him making things/working as a Sailmaker
    - Alec tries to encourage Davie e.g. to return to Sailmaking/to move elsewhere/to use his skills to create other products to sell

- Alec has accepted his dad for who he is/his likely relationship with his dad e.g. doesn't argue with Davie's (often unsatisfactory) responses/allows him to throw things of importance onto the fire

7. 1 mark for reference; 1 mark for comment (×2).

   Possible answers include:

   - "(Ah worked on the) Queen Mary (ye know)" e.g. suggests pride/sense of importance
   - "Worked on destroyers durin the war" suggests vivid memories (of usefulness)
   - Reference to list/"Made gun-covers, awnings, tarpaulins" suggests excitement at remembering detail/extent of work
   - "Made a shopping bag for yer mother"/"Made you a swing!"(1) suggests pleasure at creating gifts/ versatility of trade
   - "Wi a big sorta ..." suggests detailed memory

8. 1 mark for reference; 1 mark for comment (×2).

   Possible answers include:

   - "Nae demand" suggests skills are not needed
   - "Was different durin the War" suggests times have changed
   - "(Been goin) downhill" circumstances have worsened
   - "Yards shuttin doon" suggests no market/ employment opportunities for his trade
   - "big empty space" place of work has literally gone
   - "covered wi weeds" suggests neglect
   - "redundancy money" suggests workers have been laid off/unemployment
   - "the manmade fibres"/"usin machines"/"Got lassies daein hauf the work" suggests original trade has changed beyond recognition
   - "Dead loss" suggests no hope for old trade

9. *Possible areas for comment include:*

   From the extract:

   - negative/pessimistic/lacking motivation
   - seen to be different before the death of his wife e.g. making bags and toys, working hard as an apprentice.
   - stage directions e.g. (shrugs)
   - negative language ("backed a loser right fae the start" and "Dead loss", etc.)

   From elsewhere:

   - answers will likely focus on Davie's downwards spiral from that start of the play triggered by his inability to cope with the death of his wife, which led to gambling and drinking
   - he also struggled to cope with being a single parent to Alec, and their home situation was often unsatisfactory (e.g. provision for meals and clothing as well as the generally untidy nature of the home)
   - his employment situation changed from Sailmaker (before the play) to "tick man" to sweeper to eventually unemployed, all reflecting his decline in status/self-esteem
   - he is seen as someone who always procrastinates (e.g. doing up the yacht, tidying the house) and who cannot move on (e.g. inability to be truthful about romantic interests)

- he is seen to be intelligent (e.g. discussing literature or religion) but he never uses this or his Sailmaking skills to try and improve his situation
- he lacks the ability to be pro-active about his situation and feels that he is always unlucky
- despite these failings, he constantly encourages Alec to look for something better in life and encourages him to find this through education and employment

Candidates may choose to answer in **bullet points** in this final question, or write a number of linked statements. There is **no requirement** to write a "mini essay".

Up to 2 marks can be achieved for identifying elements of commonality as requested in the question. A further 2 marks can be achieved for **reference to the extract given**.

4 additional marks can be awarded for similar references to **at least one other part of the text.**

<u>In practice this means:</u>

Identification of commonality (e.g. theme, central relationship, importance of setting, use of imagery, development in characterisation, use of personal experience, use of narrative style or any other key element ...)

From the extract:

1 relevant reference to technique; 1 appropriate comment

OR 1 relevant reference to idea; 1 appropriate comment

OR 1 relevant reference to feature; 1 appropriate comment

OR 1 relevant reference to text; 1 appropriate comment

(maximum of 2 marks only for discussion of extract)

from at **least one other part of the text:**

as above (×2) for **up to 4 marks.**

PART A — DRAMA — *Tally's Blood* by Ann Marie Di Mambro

10. Candidates should make four key points for 1 mark each.

    Candidates may choose to make four separate summary points or may give both sides of two areas of disagreement.

    Possible answers include:

    - Rosinella thinks Hughie and Lucia are in love/ developing romantic feelings; but Massimo thinks they are just friends
    - Massimo thinks Lucia is upset about not getting to the wedding; but Rosinella thinks it's more than that
    - Massimo thinks there is no harm in her asking to go to the wedding; but Rosinella thinks it is concerning
    - Massimo thinks that Rosinella is too overbearing/ interfering/worrying too much; but Rosinella thinks she hasn't done enough to prevent this
    - Rosinella is determined to prevent their relationship developing further; but Massimo does not want to get involved in it

11. 1 mark for reference; 1 mark for comment (×2).

    Possible answers include:

    - "She's to marry an Italian" suggests Rosinella's single mindedness/insistence
    - "I don't worry enough" suggests over protectiveness

- "It's been going on before my eyes" suggests paranoia/suspicion
- "It's bad enough he's fell for her" suggests her dislike of Hughie
- "I'll soon put a stop to this before it starts" suggests her determination
- "Italians are not interested ..." suggests her prejudiced views
- short sentences suggest her blunt/frank/straight to the point nature

12. 1 mark for identifying an attitude for each character; 1 mark for supporting reference (×2).

Possible answers include:

Rosinella:

- "Are you forgetting what this country did ...?" suggests anger/bitterness/inability to let go
- "They took you" suggests sense of injustice
- "as if you were a thief" suggests she feels Massimo's treatment was terrible/unforgivable
- "I'll never get over it" suggests she feels that the trauma was too much to bear/she will hold a grudge forever

Massimo:

- "all I care about the war is that it's over" suggests he wants to move on from it/forget about it
- "I lost ma faither, ma brother" suggests that he has a deep sadness/genuine grief at loss of family
- "I lost ... four years out ma life" suggests great sadness/resentment at losing his liberty
- "everybody suffered"/"Not just us" suggests he accepts that grudges are pointless/the trauma is shared

13. *Possible areas for comment include:*

From the extract:

- Massimo is quiet, forgiving, unaware, private, patient, in love with Rosinella, etc.

From elsewhere:

- shows kindness e.g. by giving Hughie a job, offering him an ice cream van, giving Bridget money, etc.
- shows patience e.g. with Rosinella's constant comments, interfering, bossing about, etc.
- shows he is hard working e.g. works long hours in the shop while Rosinella and Lucia go out and spend, etc.
- shows love towards Rosinella e.g. romantic story of their elopement (which he re-enacts at the end of the play), affectionately calls her "Rosie", etc.
- suffers e.g. shop is attacked/has racist remarks made towards him, is taken hostage during the war, doesn't have a child of his own, etc.

Candidates may choose to answer in **bullet points** in this final question, or write a number of linked statements. There is **no requirement** to write a "mini essay".

Up to 2 marks can be achieved for identifying elements of commonality as requested in the question. A further 2 marks can be achieved for **reference to the extract given**.

4 additional marks can be awarded for similar references to at **least one other part of the text.**

In practice this means:

Identification of commonality (e.g. theme, central relationship, importance of setting, use of imagery, development in characterisation, use of personal experience, use of narrative style or any other key element ...)

From the extract:

1 relevant reference to technique; 1 appropriate comment

OR 1 relevant reference to idea; 1 appropriate comment

OR 1 relevant reference to feature; 1 appropriate comment

OR 1 relevant reference to text; 1 appropriate comment

(maximum of 2 marks only for discussion of extract)

from at **least one other part of the text:**

as above (×2) for **up to 4 marks.**

PART B — PROSE — *The Cone-Gatherers* **by Robin Jenkins**

14. Any four points for 1 mark each.

Candidates should use their own words as far as possible.

Possible answers include:

- no electric lighting
- there is not much natural light — reference to a single window
- there is little furniture — a box for a table/only two beds
- there are no soft furnishings — newspaper is used instead of a tablecloth
- they make the best of what they have
- the cones being burned — this creates a pleasant smell in the hut
- they have a simple routine e.g. they prepare the vegetables the evening before
- they prepare and eat their meal without washing/don't change their clothes
- there is little conversation/they are content with the silence/they are exhausted
- they pass the time doing simple things e.g. they have an unvarying routine

15. 1 mark for reference; 1 mark for comment (×2).

Possible answers include:

- "against his will" suggests that Duror is forced to recognise something positive about the cone-gatherers/they are at one with nature
- "final defeat" — word choice suggests that Duror is somehow seeking victory over the cone-gatherers/thinks he is superior
- "Outwardly ... inwardly" — (balanced) sentence structure OR balance OR contrast suggests the disparity between Duror's external feelings of criticism of Nazi brutality and his inner approval
- "approved" suggests in reality he hates the cone-gatherers/agrees with Hitler's attitudes
- "sensed the kinship between the carver and the creature" suggests jealousy/resentment
- "idiocy" strong word-choice used to illustrate his feelings that Calum is inferior/useless ...

- "idiots"/"imbecile" word-choice cruelly sums up Duror's criticism of Calum mentally
- "cripples"/"freak" word-choice cruelly sums up Duror's criticism of Calum physically

16. 1 mark for reference; 1 mark for comment (×2).

Possible answers include:

- "roused himself and moved away" suggests desire to distance himself
- "something unresolved" suggests lack of closure
- "never cease" suggests endless agony
- "torment" suggests Duror is suffering mentally as this conveys extreme pain/torture
- "he himself was the third" suggests sense of connection
- "he halted and looked back" suggests indecision/hesitation
- "fists tightened on the gun" suggests that Duror wishes to kill the cone-gatherers/the strength of his hatred
- "kicking" suggests feelings of violence/anger
- "disgust" suggests feelings of hatred/revulsion
- "blasting" suggests he wants to destroy them
- "icy (hand)" suggests his chilling cruelty/feelings of being controlled by fate
- reference to list suggests extreme feelings of violence/aggressive intent
- "hideous" suggests that he knows that his thoughts are wrong
- "liberating" suggests desire to be rid of them
- "fratricide" suggests murderous thoughts

17. *Possible areas for comment include:*

From the extract:

- the scene inside the cone-gatherers' hut is one of peace and tranquillity, with Neil reading the paper and Calum carving a squirrel from wood
- however, the fact that Duror is spying on the brothers and considering killing them is an example of his evil

OR

- the setting inside the hut is homely and pleasant — lamp burning/pleasant smell of burning cones; however, Duror's sympathy with the murders of "idiots and cripples" in the gas-chambers is an example of his evil thoughts

From elsewhere:

Good

- initial description of idyllic setting makes it seem like a place of tranquillity/a Garden of Eden
- Calum's goodness is referred to throughout the novel — e.g. when Neil tells him he is better than the rest of them
- Roderick's wish to befriend the cone-gatherers/ offer them a lift in the car/defend them to his mother suggests that he, too, is linked with fairness and goodness — he tells his mother "You told me yourself ... never to be quiet if I saw injustice being done."

- Roderick's intention to take the cake to the cone-gatherers as a peace-offering after the beach-hut incident shows his willingness to take responsibility for his mother's wrong
- at the end, Calum is sacrificed for the greater good — Lady Runcie-Campbell's tears represent her understanding of this

Evil

- Duror's presence in the wood is representative of the snake in the Garden of Eden — his first appearance shows him with his gun trained on Calum
- Duror's evil lies about Calum represent his wish to damage Calum's reputation and have him thrown out of the wood
- Duror's mental illness is described in metaphors of diseased/dying trees to show how such evil can destroy a strong person
- Duror's murder of Calum and his own suicide at the end illustrate the consequences of his evil

Candidates may choose to answer in **bullet points** in this final question, or write a number of linked statements. There is **no requirement** to write a "mini essay".

Up to 2 marks can be achieved for identifying elements of commonality as requested in the question. A further 2 marks can be achieved for **reference to the extract given**.

4 additional marks can be awarded for similar references to at **least one other part of the text**.

In practice this means:

Identification of commonality (e.g. theme, central relationship, importance of setting, use of imagery, development in characterisation, use of personal experience, use of narrative style or any other key element ...)

From the extract:

1 relevant reference to technique; 1 appropriate comment

OR 1 relevant reference to idea; 1 appropriate comment

OR 1 relevant reference to feature; 1 appropriate comment

OR 1 relevant reference to text; 1 appropriate comment

(maximum of 2 marks only for discussion of extract)

from at **least one other part of the text:**

as above (×2) for **up to 4 marks.**

PART B – PROSE – *The Testament of Gideon Mack* **by James Robertson**

18. Any three points for 1 mark each.

Possible answers include:

- the Devil speaks in a down to earth way
- the Devil seems vulnerable
- the Devil seems courteous/polite
- the Devil can be funny
- the Devil is the opposite to what you expect
- the Devil has some form of affection for Scotland
- the Devil is fond of telling stories about his travels/ adventures/impressions of people and places
- the Devil enjoys the depressive nature of the people in Scotland

- the Devil likes the terrible weather (in Scotland)
- the Devil is an astute commentator on changes in society
- the Devil subverts biblical texts/ideas
- the Devil can be changeable

19. 1 mark for reference; 1 mark for comment.

Possible answers include:

- "I made no further protest"/"I couldn't help it" suggests contrition
- "terrible arm" suggests terror
- "I shrank away" suggests avoidance
- "terrified" suggests intense fear
- "clutching" suggests tension
- "I closed my eyes" suggests trepidation

20. Any three points for 1 mark each.

Possible answers include:

- Devil puts his hand in the fire; until it is very hot; then he comes towards Mack's leg with the hot arm
- Mack feels a strange sensation in his leg
- the Devil's hand is placed under Mack's skin
- the skin looks like it is burning/feels like it is on fire
- the Devil manipulates the bone; back in alignment; and sticks it back together
- the process is painless

21. Candidates must address two different aspects.

1 mark for reference; 1 mark for comment (×2).

Possible answers include:

- annoyed/grumpy or similar shown by "sparked up a bit"/"snapped"
- assertive/taking control or similar shown by repetition of "don't think"
- nostalgic/warm or similar shown by stories of North Berwick and/or Auchtermuchty/(repetition of) "I like Scotland"/any example of why he likes Scotland
- sad/down in the dumps or similar shown by "morose"/"fed up"
- cheerful/happy or similar shown by "brightened"
- vulnerable/needy or similar shown by "please"/"I'd like to"
- focused/intent or similar shown by "(intense) concentration"/"fully three minutes"/general comment on his focus when fixing the leg

22. Candidates should identify one aspect of Mack's character in this extract and go on to discuss how this is developed elsewhere in the novel. It should be at least implied that the character traits are as a result of meeting the Devil.

Accept also events which follow the meeting in the cave which are a direct result of the meeting e.g. Catherine's funeral, his seeming madness, his being 'struck off', his disappearance but links must be made in the explanation to the meeting with the Devil.

Possible aspects of character include:

- arrogance – e.g. he has suffered a near death experience as well as meeting the devil, and survived, which makes him feel untouchable, all

powerful or similar as exemplified elsewhere in the novel in his dealings with the community, interested parties, etc. (before the meeting with the Devil, Mack is portrayed as a weak and cowardly character)

- self-righteousness – e.g. he has seen things that others have not and he wants to tell everyone about this as exemplified at Catherine's funeral
- argumentative/contrariness – e.g. refusal to back down in the face of huge opposition later in the book, resulting in him being excommunicated
- air of mystery – e.g. he keeps himself to himself and/or eventually disappears completely

Candidates may choose to answer in **bullet points** in this final question, or write a number of linked statements. There is **no requirement** to write a "mini essay".

Up to 2 marks can be achieved for identifying elements of commonality as requested in the question. A further 2 marks can be achieved for **reference to the extract given**.

4 additional marks can be awarded for similar references to at **least one other part of the text**.

In practice this means:

Identification of commonality (e.g. theme, central relationship, importance of setting, use of imagery, development in characterisation, use of personal experience, use of narrative style or any other key element …)

From the extract:

1 relevant reference to technique; 1 appropriate comment

OR 1 relevant reference to idea; 1 appropriate comment

OR 1 relevant reference to feature; 1 appropriate comment

OR 1 relevant reference to text; 1 appropriate comment

(**maximum of 2 marks only for discussion of extract**)

from at **least one other part of the text:**

as above (×2) for **up to 4 marks**.

PART B – PROSE – *Kidnapped* by Robert Louis Stevenson

23. Any four points for 1 mark each.

Possible answers include:

- the sun rises and Alan and David see where they are
- Alan is worried that they will be found at this location
- Alan leaps over the river
- David follows Alan
- they have a large jump to make from the middle rock to the other bank of the river
- David is scared
- Alan is angry at him
- Alan gives David alcohol to calm him
- David initially does not make it
- Alan takes hold of him and pulls him ashore

24. (a) 1 mark for reference; 1 mark for comment.

Possible answers include:

- "ran harder than ever" suggests no one can catch him
- "Alan looked neither to the right or the left" suggests he's oblivious to danger

- "jumped clean upon the middle rock" suggests athletic prowess
- "that rock was small" suggests difficulty doesn't faze him

(b) 1 mark for reference; 1 mark for comment.

Possible answers include:

- "this horrible place" suggests David's unhappiness with the setting
- "horrid thundering" suggests David's anxiety
- "made my belly quake" suggests fear
- "scarce time" suggests panic
- "to understand the peril" suggests necessity of acting quickly

25. 1 mark for sentence structure feature/reference; 1 mark for relevant comment on feature/reference; 1 mark for word choice example; 1 mark for relevant comment on word choice.

Possible answers include:

Sentence structure

- repetition of "I"/repetition of first person pronoun and/or associated verb emphasises dramatic action/ gives a sense of immediacy
- repetition of "slipped" emphasises the danger and drama as David tries to jump the river
- long sentence (lines 25–28) emphasises the drama of the action through explanation of David's thought process as he faces danger
- long sentence (lines 25–28)/list emphasis of drama through list of actions in long sentence/number of dangers
- listing [any examples from lines 25–28 in particular]; "these slipped, caught again, slipped again"

OR

- "[Alan seized me,] first by the hair, then by the collar" provides a powerful dramatic effect in their speed and immediacy

Word choice

- "alone" emphasises that David may feel isolated and fearful at this point, hence dramatic
- "flung" has connotations of throwing himself with some force, possibly desperate
- "anger" emphasises his strong emotional state
- "despair" connotations of hopelessness which creates dramatic mood
- "seized" emphasises the desperate dramatic action taken by Alan
- "great strain" emphasises the effort required to save David and enhances the drama of the moment
- "dragged" emphasises the weight and dramatic struggle Alan had to bring David to the bank of the river

26. *Possible areas for comment include:*

- Alan's prowess in the roundhouse conflict on the Covenant
- Alan's gift of the silver button to David
- Alan's showing David the political realities of the Scottish Highlands

- Alan assisting David in his journey back to Edinburgh
- Alan getting the Balquidder safe house
- Alan convincing girl to row them over the River Forth
- Alan's contribution in trapping Ebenezer at the end of the novel
- Alan's friendship enhances David's self-confidence
- Alan's role in David's life helps in David maturing into a man

Candidates may choose to answer in **bullet points** in this final question, or write a number of linked statements. There is **no requirement** to write a "mini essay".

Up to 2 marks can be achieved for identifying elements of commonality as requested in the question. A further 2 marks can be achieved for **reference to the extract given**.

4 additional marks can be awarded for similar references to at **least one other part of the text**.

In practice this means:

Identification of commonality (e.g. theme, central relationship, importance of setting, use of imagery, development in characterisation, use of personal experience, use of narrative style or any other key element …)

From the extract:

1 relevant reference to technique; 1 appropriate comment

OR 1 relevant reference to idea; 1 appropriate comment

OR 1 relevant reference to feature; 1 appropriate comment

OR 1 relevant reference to text; 1 appropriate comment

(maximum of 2 marks only for discussion of extract)

from at **least one other part of the text:**

as above (×2) for **up to 4 marks**.

PART B – PROSE – *The Crater* by Iain Crichton Smith

27. 1 mark for reference; 1 mark for comment (×2).

Possible answers include:

- "squirmed" suggests unease/discomfort/difficulty in moving
- (blunt statement) "I am frightened" highlights the danger he faced
- repetition (of "fear") conveys the overpowering nature of his feelings
- "grey figures" suggests his terror of the unknown/ unfamiliar
- "darkness" conveys his helplessness/despair about his situation
- enemy "crawling beneath" suggests his deep-rooted/ inner emotions
- spider's web suggests his horror of being caught/ trapped/killed by the enemy

28. Any four points for 1 mark each.

Possible answers include:

- the commotion/confusion ("thrustings and flashes")
- the difficulty in determining reality from illusion ("saw or imagined he saw")
- the threat from explosives and weapons ("Mills bombs/bayonets")

- the vermin ("scurryings...rats")
- the individual danger of face-to-face combat ("face towered above him")
- the disgusting conditions ("terrible stink")
- the brutality/violence ("flowing of blood")
- the likelihood of being killed

29. Candidates should identify an example of sentence structure and comment on how this conveys the danger faced by the men.

1 mark for reference; 1 mark for comment.

Possible answers include:

- single word sentence "Back" suggests the pressure of the moment
- repetition of "back" conveys the frantic atmosphere/ unsafe/unstable environment
- minor sentence "Over the parapet" shows the threat/risk/exposed/fragile nature of their position
- inversion of "crouched" highlights their vulnerability/ helplessness (in the face of enemy fire)
- repetition of "and" **OR** list of actions "crouched/run/ scrambled" suggests the many difficulties in reaching safety

30. 1 mark for reference; 1 mark for comment.

Possible answers include:

- "there is no point" the men's realisation of their gloomy predicament
- "could not tell the expression" suggests their loss of connection/numbness about their situation
- "shells still falling" suggests the ceaseless fighting
- "dead moons" suggests the lack of hope/dark world they inhabit

31. *Possible areas for comment include:*

- "Mother and Son" — the impact of the mother's words e.g. "her bitter barbs passed over him...Most often however they stung him and stood quivering in his flesh" to convey the destructive nature of their relationship
- "The Telegram" — The symbolism of birds e.g. "domestic bird...aquiline ...buzzard" to show the contrasting nature of the two women/convey the theme of sacrifice/constraints of small community/ isolation/effects of war
- "The Red Door" — The many references to colour/ symbolism of the door/description of the landscape e.g. "the earth was painted with an unearthly glow and the sea was like a strange volume" to highlight Murdo's growing realisation that he does not have to conform
- "In Church" — The religious symbolism and language e.g. "gods were carelessly punching" to convey the devastating effects/futility of war

Candidates may choose to answer in **bullet points** in this final question, or write a number of linked statements. There is **no requirement** to write a "mini essay".

Up to 2 marks can be achieved for identifying elements of commonality as requested in the question. A further 2 marks can be achieved for **reference to the extract given.**

4 additional marks can be awarded for similar references to at **least one other part of the text.**

In practice this means:

Identification of commonality (e.g. theme, central relationship, importance of setting, use of imagery, development in characterisation, use of personal experience, use of narrative style or any other key element ...)

From the extract:

1 relevant reference to technique; 1 appropriate comment

OR 1 relevant reference to idea; 1 appropriate comment

OR 1 relevant reference to feature; 1 appropriate comment

OR 1 relevant reference to text; 1 appropriate comment

(maximum of 2 marks only for discussion of extract)

from at **least one other part of the text:**

as above (×2) for **up to 4 marks.**

PART B — PROSE — *Zimmerobics* by Anne Donovan

32. Two points for 1 mark each.

Possible answers include:

- resigned/uneasy/reluctant/sceptical at the start
- cautiously optimistic
- increasingly confident
- completely involved/very pleased with herself/ happy/convinced of its benefits

33. 1 mark for reference; 1 mark for comment.

Possible answers include:

- "Creaking sounds"/"creaky old joints" suggests lack of agility
- "shuffled in most cases" suggests caution/slowness
- "(old and) decrepit" suggests decay/decline
- "hirpled" suggests difficulty of movement

34. 1 mark for reference; 1 mark for comment (×2).

Possible answers include:

- "pleasant tingling in my limbs" suggests enjoyment
- "I became quite proficient" suggests pride in developing skill
- "It was brilliant" suggests enthusiasm
- "(my body) still worked" suggests relief/wonderment
- "the memory of the exercise class lingered" suggests long lasting impact
- "I felt better/as though someone had oiled all the creaky old joints" suggests physical benefits
- "a pleasant ache/an ache of life" suggests love of life

35. 1 mark for reference; 1 mark for comment (×2).

Possible answers include:

- reference to school uniform suggests comic embarrassment
- "Cheryl bounced" suggests over-energetic movement, or similar comment on humorous connotations of word choice
- ("wearing a pair of trainers that made her) feet look like horse's hooves" suggests clumsiness/ ungainliness, or similar comment on the incongruity of the image applied to a fitness instructor

- detailed description of the outfit, over the top attention to detail
- "I hope she doesn't need to go to the toilet in a hurry" humorous comment on impractical nature of outfit
- lengthy/detailed/exaggerated description of routine/ understanding of implication of high level of skill in contrast with the limited activity actually done
- parenthetical comment/"(well, shuffled in most cases)" plus comment on mocking tone/self-deprecating humour
- hyperbole/"boldly" to describe a simple action
- juxtaposition of "boldly" and "zimmer-frames" incongruous nature of the two terms
- word choice/"shuffled"/"hirpled" in contrast with words you would expect to describe exercise movements, implying energy, grace or skill

36. *Possible areas for comment include:*

- "All that Glisters" — any aspect or development of Clare's relationship with her father such as her desire to make her father happy with the card she makes at school; Clare's concern for her father's deteriorating health; the closeness between Clare and her father shown through her explanation of "subtle", and the way she defies her aunt at the end of the story, to do what her father would have liked; Clare's creativity shown through how she applies the pens to card early in the story and to herself at the end; Clare's determination to obtain the pens and the sacrifice she is prepared to make to afford them; Clare's shocked reaction to her father's death; the conflict between Clare and the shop assistant and her aunt. Use of first person narrative/dialect/informal register/simple word choice to bring authenticity/ help the reader understand Clare's thoughts and feelings

- "Virtual Pals" — use of emails/first person narrative allows the reader to understand Siobhan's thoughts/ to see her becoming more confident. Use of simple sentence structure, word choice and dialect reflect her age/experience/interests, etc. Themes such as friendship and trust, and boyfriend issues are typical teenage concerns, creating authenticity

- "Dear Santa" — use of first person narrative/ dialect/informal register/simple word choice to reveal Alison's feelings (e.g. unloved by her mother, overlooked by her father, jealous of her sister and worthless overall), and to show Alison is growing up and changing in the references to Santa. Use of imagery to reveal her feelings for her mother, her sister, and about herself. Use of example/anecdote to show her feelings about Katie/herself

- "A Chitterin Bite" — use of contrasting registers to highlight differences in character between young and adult Mary. Use of informal register to reflect Mary's character as a child. Use of standard English to show adult Mary has changed. Use of two time frames to allow the reader to see the change in how Mary reacts to being let down as a child and how she reacts as an adult. Use of symbolism of the "chitterin bite" to show Mary's character changing — initially, comforting, associated with friendship, then chokes her, associated with rejection, then a symbol for her revenge and ability to move on

- "Away in a Manger" — use of dialect to make Sandra's and Amy's characters convincing; use of dialogue to create convincing parent child relationship; use of dialogue to demonstrate love between Sandra and Amy; Sandra's and Amy's different attitudes to the nativity to show the difference between a child's and an adult's perspective

Candidates may choose to answer in **bullet points** in this final question, or write a number of linked statements. There is **no requirement** to write a "mini essay".

Up to 2 marks can be achieved for identifying elements of commonality as requested in the question. A further 2 marks can be achieved for **reference to the extract given.**

4 additional marks can be awarded for similar references to at **least one other part of the text.**

In practice this means:

Identification of commonality (e.g. theme, central relationship, importance of setting, use of imagery, development in characterisation, use of personal experience, use of narrative style or any other key element ...)

From the extract:

1 relevant reference to technique; 1 appropriate comment

OR 1 relevant reference to idea; 1 appropriate comment

OR 1 relevant reference to feature; 1 appropriate comment

OR 1 relevant reference to text; 1 appropriate comment

(maximum of 2 marks only for discussion of extract)

from at **least one other part of the text:**

as above (×2) for **up to 4 marks.**

PART C — POETRY — *War Photographer* by Carol Ann Duffy

37. 1 mark for reference; 1 mark for comment.

Possible answers include:

- "darkroom"/"finally alone" suggests confessional
- "suffering" suggests passion/pain/key concern of religion, etc.
- "(set out in) ordered rows" suggests lines of pews/ bibles, etc.
- "The only light is red"/"softly glows" suggests ever-present illumination (often from a candle) in some churches
- "preparing to intone" suggests that the photographer's tasks (in developing photographs) reminds the poet of a priest's ritual
- "Mass" suggests religious ceremony
- "All flesh is grass" is a Biblical reference

38. Candidates should include one example from each side (home country & countries visited).

1 mark for reference; 1 mark for comment (×2).

Possible answers include:

Home country:

- "Home again" suggests relief at returning/comfort/ security
- "Rural England" suggests peaceful countryside

- short/minor sentence (of "Rural England.") suggests isolation from harm/conflict, etc.
- "ordinary pain" suggests any discomforts are bearable
- "simple weather" suggests climate is constant/predictable/not dramatic

Countries visited:

- "explode beneath the feet" suggests violence/unexpected, dramatic happenings
- "running" suggests imminent danger
- "running children" even young people are under threat
- "nightmare" suggests terror/fear/sleeplessness
- "nightmare heat" suggests discomfort/reference to napalm attacks/extreme weather

39. 1 mark for reference; 1 mark for comment (×2).

Possible answers include:

- "Something is happening."/dramatic short sentence suggests emergence of strong recollection
- "twist (before his eyes)" suggests painful image
- "half-formed ghost" suggests photographer is haunted by memories
- "cries (of this man's wife)" suggests potent/strong/disturbing sounds
- "blood" suggests disturbing/violent image
- "stained into foreign dust" suggests permanent impression

40. Two points for 1 mark each. Candidates should use their own words.

Possible answers include:

- only a small selection of the photographs are revealed to the public
- futility of photographer's effort
- readers don't pay sufficient attention to the scale of suffering/carry on with lives regardless
- readers are insufficiently emotionally engaged
- photographer has become hardened
- the world has become numb to conflict

41. *Possible areas for comment include:*

- "Havisham" — main character suffers due to painful memories of wedding day
- "Originally" — suffering due to moving to unfamiliar place. Suffering perhaps due to questions of identity. Also idea of moving on from suffering and revising identity
- "Mrs Midas" — main character suffers due to behaviour/obsessions of her partner
- "Valentine" — potential pain and suffering caused by love
- "Anne Hathaway" — loss felt at Shakespeare's absence from her life. She is left just with memories

Candidates may choose to answer in **bullet points** in this final question, or write a number of linked statements. There is **no requirement** to write a "mini essay".

Up to 2 marks can be achieved for identifying elements of commonality as requested in the question. A further 2 marks can be achieved for **reference to the extract given**.

4 additional marks can be awarded for similar references to at **least one other poem by Duffy**.

In practice this means:

Identification of commonality (e.g. theme, central relationship, importance of setting, use of imagery, development in characterisation, use of personal experience, use of narrative style or any other key element …)

From the extract:

1 relevant reference to technique; 1 appropriate comment

OR 1 relevant reference to idea; 1 appropriate comment

OR 1 relevant reference to feature; 1 appropriate comment

OR 1 relevant reference to text; 1 appropriate comment

(maximum of 2 marks only for discussion of extract)

from at **least one other poem:**

as above (×2) for **up to 4 marks**.

PART C — POETRY — *Trio* **by Edwin Morgan**

42. 1 mark for reference; 1 mark for comment.

Possible answers include:

- "quickly" suggests vitality/liveliness
- "Christmas lights" suggests festive/celebration/happy time of year
- "new (guitar)" suggests happiness of giving/receiving
- "(very young) baby" suggests happiness of new birth
- "(the three of them are) laughing" suggests happiness/enjoyment
- "(their breath) rises" suggests uplifting moment
- "(in a cloud of) happiness" suggests delight/enjoyment
- "'Wait till he sees this but!'" suggests eagerness/delight

43. 1 mark for reference; 1 mark for comment.

Possible answers include:

- "baby" suggests new birth
- "white (shawl)" suggests purity
- "bright (eyes)" suggests clarity/purity
- "fresh (sweet cake)" suggests newness/unspoiled
- "milky (plastic cover)" suggests whiteness
- "silver tinsel tape"/"sprig of mistletoe" suggest Christmas time, which is a celebration of new birth

44. 1 mark for reference; 1 mark for comment (×2).

Possible answers include:

- "… powerless before you" suggests that nothing can stop them
- "you put paid" suggests that they conquer
- "(put paid) to fate" suggests that even a seemingly unstoppable force (fate) cannot stand in the way of them
- "… it abdicates" suggests the group compels the opposition to give up
- "Monsters" suggests that the group is prepared to stand up to fearsome opposition
- "(Monsters of the year) go blank" suggests that opposition freezes/has no solution

- "are scattered back" suggests that the opposition surrenders
- "can't bear" suggests that nothing can stand/endure the force of the group
- "march" suggests that the group has the strength of an army

45. 1 mark for reference; 1 mark for comment (×2).

Possible answers include:

- "yet not vanished" suggests the group will not disappear/will keep going/they will be there in spirit but not physically there
- "for in their arms they wind the life of men and beasts" suggests that the group is important to/stand for all nature/humanity/continuity/persistence
- "music" suggests celebration, etc.
- "laughter (ringing them round)" suggests happiness
- "at the end of this winter's day" suggests that the group represents the end of winter/moving on to Spring, etc.

46. *Possible areas for comment include:*

- "Hyena" — the setting of African dry lands is important in establishing how the hyena fits in with/relates to its environment
- "In the Snack-bar" — the setting of the Snack-bar is crucial to Morgan's depiction of the difficulties faced by the old man
- "Good Friday" — the setting of the bus/Glasgow is central to Morgan's central concerns of class differences, etc. Setting in time of Easter is central to concerns of religion
- "Winter" — the setting of Bingham's Pond/West End of Glasgow is important in Morgan's exploration of themes of death and time
- "Slate" — Morgan uses the setting of Scotland's mountains/landscape to consider themes of time/nationhood, etc.

Candidates may choose to answer in **bullet points** in this final question, or write a number of linked statements. There is **no requirement** to write a "mini essay".

Up to 2 marks can be achieved for identifying elements of commonality as requested in the question. A further 2 marks can be achieved for **reference to the extract given.**

4 additional marks can be awarded for similar references to at **least one other poem by Morgan.**

<u>In practice this means:</u>

Identification of commonality (e.g. theme, central relationship, importance of setting, use of imagery, development in characterisation, use of personal experience, use of narrative style or any other key element ...)

From the extract:

1 relevant reference to technique; 1 appropriate comment

OR 1 relevant reference to idea; 1 appropriate comment

OR 1 relevant reference to feature; 1 appropriate comment

OR 1 relevant reference to text; 1 appropriate comment

(maximum of 2 marks only for discussion of extract)

from at **least one other poem:**

as above (×2) for **up to 4 marks.**

PART C — POETRY — *Aunt Julia* by Norman MacCaig

47. 1 mark for reference; 1 mark for comment.

NB: Do not award a mark for "frustration" as this is in the question.

Possible answers include:

- "(Aunt Julia spoke) Gaelic" suggests that there is a language barrier between Aunt Julia and the poet
- "very loud and very fast" repetition emphasises the difficulties of understanding
- "loud" suggests annoyance at high volume
- "fast" speed caused difficulties in understanding
- "I could not...I could not" repetition emphasises the fact that the poet is conscious of his own inadequacies in communicating with Aunt Julia
- "(I could not) answer her" suggests poet's inability to reply/communicate
- "(I could not) understand her" suggests poet's lack of comprehension

48. 1 mark for reference; 1 mark for comment (×2).

NB: Do not reward the same analytical comment given twice for two different references.

Possible answers include:

- "(She wore) men's boots" suggests her unconventional dress/work ethic
- "(when she wore) any" suggests poverty/hardiness
- "strong (foot)" suggests physical capabilities
- "stained with peat" suggests lack of vanity/work ethic/she is at one with the land
- "paddling with...while her right hand" suggests dexterity/high level of skill
- "marvellously (out of the air)" suggests almost magical abilities
- "Hers"/"(Hers) was the only house" suggests uniqueness/sense of security
- "crickets being friendly" suggests peace/contentment
- "(She was) buckets"/"water flouncing into them" suggests plenty/abundance of natural resources/she was almost "elemental"
- "She was winds ..." suggests that she represents the island gales
- "(She was) brown eggs" suggests nature/crofting life
- "black skirts" suggests she represented typical island dress of the time
- "(keeper of) threepennybits" suggests habits of economy/savings/combating poverty

49. 1 mark for reference; 1 mark for comment (×2).

Possible answers include:

- "(By the time) I had learned a little" suggests regret at time passing/lateness of learning
- "silenced" is associated with death/contrasts with earlier volume of Aunt Julia
- "absolute black" suggests death/darkness/oblivion/loss
- "sandy grave" suggests death

50. 1 mark for reference from specified lines; 1 mark for reference from elsewhere/comment on ideas or technique. Points/references must match up.

    Possible answers include:

    - "getting angry, getting angry" echoes repetition employed at various points in the poem/ identification of an example of repetition e.g. "very loud and very fast"

    - "getting angry" echoes dissatisfaction expressed earlier in the poem/identification of example e.g. "I could not ... etc."

    - "questions unanswered" echoes earlier communication problems/identification of example e.g. "I could not understand her", etc.

    - "But I hear her still" echoes earlier reference to her voice/reference to her ever present nature

    - "seagull's voice" echoes earlier reference to "very loud", "loud", "fast", etc.

    - "peatscrapes and lazy beds" echoes earlier reference to landscape/"stained with peat"

51. *Possible areas for comment include:*

    - "Visiting Hour" — "white cave of forgetfulness," "distance of pain," "neither she nor I can cross," "books that will not be read", etc. are all references to being separated from someone close

    - "Assisi" — the beggar is kept separate from/outside of the church and/or the guide's tour of the church

    - "Memorial" — separation caused by death. Constant reminders of separation from surroundings, etc.

    - "Sounds of the day" — separation made potent by sounds/silences. Long-lasting impact of separation ("quietest fire in the world")

    - "Basking Shark" — realisation that humans have separated themselves from nature/origins

    Candidates may choose to answer in **bullet points** in this final question, or write a number of linked statements. There is **no requirement** to write a "mini essay".

    Up to 2 marks can be achieved for identifying elements of commonality as requested in the question. A further 2 marks can be achieved for **reference to the extract given.**

    4 additional marks can be awarded for similar references to at **least one other poem by MacCaig.**

    <u>In practice this means:</u>

    Identification of commonality (e.g. theme, central relationship, importance of setting, use of imagery, development in characterisation, use of personal experience, use of narrative style or any other key element ...)

    From the extract:

    1 relevant reference to technique; 1 appropriate comment

    OR 1 relevant reference to idea; 1 appropriate comment

    OR 1 relevant reference to feature; 1 appropriate comment

    OR 1 relevant reference to text; 1 appropriate comment

    (maximum of 2 marks only for discussion of extract)

    from at **least one other poem:**

    as above (×2) for **up to 4 marks.**

PART C — POETRY — *Bed* by Jackie Kay

52. 1 mark for reference; 1 mark for comment (×2).

    NB: Do not reward the same analytical comment given twice for two different references.

    Possible answers include:

    - "(Am a) burden (tae her)" suggests that the speaker is aware of her own dependency

    - "Stuck (here)" suggests the speaker feels trapped

    - "(big) blastit (bed)" suggests that the speaker is cursing the fact that she is confined to bed

    - "big blastit bed" alliteration emphasises speaker's annoyance at being confined in bed

    - "year in, year oot" repetition emphasises monotony/ endlessness of existence

    - "ony saint wuid complain" suggests speaker's patience has been stretched

    - "A' wish she didnae huv tae dae" suggests speaker's embarrassment at/awareness of dependency

    - "(Am her) wean (noo)" suggests speaker feels she is treated like a baby/is dependent

    - "ma great tent o' nappy" suggests speaker is embarrassed about undignified aspects of her current life

    - "champed egg in a cup"/"mashed tattie" suggests speaker is critical of the food she has to eat/is given

    - "Aw the treats ... she's gieing me" suggests the speaker is unhappy about the role reversal with her daughter

    - "A' dinny ken whit happened" suggests speaker's confusion over her current circumstances

    - "We dinny talk any mair" suggests speaker's regret at loss of communication

    - "the blethers ha been plucked oot o'us" suggests speaker is aware of lack of communication/ conversation

53. 1 mark for reference; 1 mark for comment (×2).

    NB: Do not reward the same analytical comment given twice for two different references.

    Possible answers include:

    - "like some skinny chicken" suggests reduced physical state/loss of humanity or individuality

    - "skinny" suggests weight loss

    - "ma skin ... loose flap noo" suggests skin is in poor condition

    - "A' took pride in ma guid smooth skin" suggests contrast of current state of physical appearance with former state

    - "Aw A' dae is sit an look oot this windae" suggests boredom

    - "A've seen hale generations graw up" suggests being left behind

    - "... this same windae" suggests length of time in one place/lack of variety

    - "that's no seen a lick o' paint fir donkeys" suggests neglect

54. 1 mark for reference; 1 mark for comment.

Possible answers include:

- "so am telt"/"hauf the time A' dinny believe her" suggests lack of trust between mother and daughter

- "My dochter says 'Awright mother?'" suggests lack of genuine interest/concern from her daughter

- "(haunds me) a thin broth or puried neep" suggests speaker's unhappiness with the food her daughter brings her

- "an A say 'Aye fine,'" suggests response is not genuine

- "great heaving sigh"/"ma crabbit tut"/"ma froon"/"A' pu' ma cardie tight" suggests displeasure

- "ma auld loose lips" suggests speaking without thought

55. Two points for 1 mark each. Candidates should use their own words.

Gloss of:

- "biding time" e.g. waiting to die

- "Time is whit A' hauld between the soft bits o' ma thumbs" e.g. she knows that her time is limited/not much left

- "the skeleton underneath ma night goon" e.g. she is aware that death is approaching

- "the glaring selfish moon" e.g. she takes no joy from nature/the world

- "this drab wee prison" e.g. she feels trapped/lack of freedom

- "A'll be gone and how wull she feel" e.g. she has doubts over her daughter's emotions/attitude towards her

- "No that ... Grateful" e.g. part of her wants her daughter to appreciate her more/her thoughts have become bitter

56. *Possible areas for comment include:*

- "Gap Year" — a mother reacting to/trying to adapt to her son having left home/being far away

- "My Grandmother's Houses" — speaker reflects on the impact of moving house for her grandmother

- "Lucozade" — change in relationships caused by illness/hospitalisation

- "Divorce" — speaker desperately seeks change in relationship with parents

- "Keeping Orchids" — speaker reflects on changing relationship with mother

Candidates may choose to answer in **bullet points** in this final question, or write a number of linked statements. There is **no requirement** to write a "mini essay".

Up to 2 marks can be achieved for identifying elements of commonality as requested in the question. A further 2 marks can be achieved for **reference to the extract given**.

4 additional marks can be awarded for similar references to at **least one other poem by Kay**.

In practice this means:

Identification of commonality (e.g. theme, central relationship, importance of setting, use of imagery, development in characterisation, use of personal experience, use of narrative style or any other key element ...)

From the extract:

1 relevant reference to technique; 1 appropriate comment

OR 1 relevant reference to idea; 1 appropriate comment

OR 1 relevant reference to feature; 1 appropriate comment

OR 1 relevant reference to text; 1 appropriate comment

(maximum of 2 marks only for discussion of extract)

from at **least one other poem:**

as above (×2) for **up to 4 marks.**

SECTION 2 – CRITICAL ESSAY

Please see the assessment criteria for the Critical Essay on page 123.

NATIONAL 5 ENGLISH 2018

READING FOR UNDERSTANDING, ANALYSIS AND EVALUATION

1. Any two points, for a maximum of 2 marks.

   Possible answers include:

   - 'Mini Master' glossed by e.g. he seems very important/seems to be the boss
   - 'photogenic' glossed by e.g. he is attractive/nice to look at
     NB Do not accept any references to looking good in a photo
   - 'spirit of the place' glossed by e.g. he is the heart and soul of the shop/immediately associated with the shop/seems to embody its essence
   - 'gives you approximately five seconds to impress him'/'to impress him, otherwise he goes right back to sleep' glossed by e.g. you don't have much time to engage his interest

2. Any five points, for a maximum of 5 marks.

   Possible answers include:

   - '(keep you in check by) making you work for their love' glossed by e.g. ensuring you have to try hard to gain their affection
   - 'apex (of domesticated pets)' glossed by e.g. they are at the very top (of the rank order of pets)/they are the very best
   - 'co-owner'/'manager' glossed by e.g. cat seems to be in charge/the boss
   - 'security' glossed by e.g. cats seem to offer protection
   - 'abiding conscience (of the place)' glossed by e.g. they seem to have a moral compass/know the difference between right and wrong
   - '(seem) above it all' glossed by e.g. they are proud/aloof/superior
   - 'force you to contemplate things' glossed by e.g. they make you think
     NB 'force' must be glossed
   - 'they just seem smarter than they're letting on' glossed by e.g. they are more intelligent than they appear
     NB Do not accept idea that cats are clever on its own
   - 'know everything but won't tell' glossed by e.g. they are aware of all that's going on but they can keep a secret
     NB Do not accept idea that cats are clever on its own

3. Any four points, for a maximum of 4 marks.

   Possible answers include:

   - 'ancestors were worshipped as gods'/'the popular idea that Egyptians worshipped them'
     glossed by e.g. cats used to be treated as religious icons/treated with the utmost respect/were the subjects of adoration/were praised
     NB Do not accept loved on its own without further qualification
   - 'we grovelled in caves and painted our bodies blue' glossed by e.g. humans seemed primitive in comparison with cats/inferior

   - 'if you even accidentally killed a cat, you'd be sentenced to death' glossed by e.g. harming a cat/ending a cat's life (by mistake) would have serious consequences/was punished severely
     NB Do not accept lifts of 'killed' or 'death'
   - 'Cats were often adorned with jewels' glossed by e.g. cats were decorated with/were dressed/wore precious stones
     NB Do not accept jewellery
   - '(fed) meals …well, tinned cat food' glossed by e.g. cats were given fancy/quality food
   - 'They were sometimes mummified' glossed by e.g. bodies of cats were preserved/cats were accorded same burial rites as important people
   - 'grieving owners shaved off their eyebrows' glossed by e.g. death of cats was marked in special ways/affected their owners deeply
   - 'Bastet, the deity,…Egyptians worshipped them.' glossed by e.g. even the gods aspired to be cats

4. Any one pair, OR two correct selections covering different directions, for a maximum of 2 marks.

   Possible answers include:

   - '(sort of) treatment' OR 'time of pharaoh' looks back to 'Egyptian society' OR 'adorned with jewels' OR 'fed meals …' OR 'sometimes mummified' OR 'worshipped them' OR paraphrase of any of the above
   - '(cats) haven't really moved on' looks forward to 'carry themselves in a stately manner' OR 'demand you treat them with a certain amount of reverence' OR '(doing a good job of) petting them' OR 'what they like and what displeases them' OR paraphrase of any of the above
   - '(sort of) treatment' OR 'time of Pharaoh' looks back '(cats) haven't really moved on' looks forward

5. 1 mark for any one reference/identification of structural technique; 1 mark for comment.

   Possible answers include:

   - 'My cats certainly do.'/short sentence demonstrates emphatic nature of cats' intentions
   - 'shooting me a look, letting out a sad meow, and then instigating a showdown'/three-part structure/climactic construction/list emphasises different things cats do to show their displeasure (at being moved)
   - 'And their favourite places in my house? Among my books.'/question and answer construction emphasises fact that cats decide where they want to be/position themselves
   - 'And their favourite places in my house?'/question emphasises that cats choose for themselves
   - 'Among my books.'/minor sentence emphasises the place cats like best

6. 1 mark for any one reference; 1 mark for comment (×2), for a maximum of 4 marks.

   NB Candidates must make two distinct selections. This distinction could be made through either presentation or comment.

Possible answers include:

- 'trained' suggests e.g. cats were taught (what to do)
- 'pests' suggests e.g. cats got rid of destructive creatures
- 'lost' suggests e.g. without cats knowledge would have disappeared
- '(four-legged) protectors' suggests e.g. cats looked after Egyptian writing/were the guardians of the writing
- 'guarding (the temples)' suggests e.g. cats defended Egyptian writing
- 'intruders' suggests e.g. cats stopped invaders

7. 1 mark for any one reference; 1 mark for comment (×2), for a maximum of 4 marks.

Possible answers include:

Word choice:

- 'cartoonesque'/'Tom and Jerry' suggests e.g. he disagrees with the stereotypical/unrealistic/ representation of cats
- 'dumb (cat)' suggests e.g. that the writer has the opposite view/is used in an ironic sense
- '(always) foiled' suggests e.g. that writer thinks whatever the cat does it cannot win
- 'tiny adversary' suggests e.g. ridiculous elevation of mouse/is used in an ironic sense
- '(little) pests' suggests e.g. mice should be considered as undesirable creatures
- 'gnawing'/'gnawing on our possessions' suggests e.g. continuous destruction/suggests that mice ruin our things
- 'spreading'/'spreading disease' suggests e.g. mice are causing harm everywhere/are dangerous (to our health)
- 'unfair' suggests e.g. cats are unjustly treated

Sentence structure:

- 'It's unfair.'/short sentence emphasises e.g. writer's opinion that cats are treated without due respect
- contrast of long and short sentences gives e.g. emphatic weight to writer's opinion that treatment of cats is unjust

Tone:

- reference to appropriate tone e.g. 'like we're supposed to' creates a mocking tone

8. Any five points, for a maximum of 5 marks.

Possible answers include:

- 'Look to Russia' glossed by e.g. it all started in Russia OR 'decree issued by Empress Elizabeth' glossed by e.g. (cats were subject to) a special order
- 'to protect the treasures contained within (the Museum) from rats' glossed by e.g. cats were employed to stop rats from ruining the valuables (of the museum)
  NB Both 'protect' and 'treasures' must be glossed here

- 'Europeans still sure that rats caused the Black Death' glossed by e.g. rats were blamed for the Plague OR 'rat catchers unable to stop rodents from overrunning' glossed by e.g. the rat population was out of control
  NB 'caused' must be glossed
- 'the British government started to encourage libraries to keep cats in order to bring down populations of (book-loving) vermin' glossed by e.g. the use of cats was recommended in UK libraries to deal with the rats
  NB 'encouraged' must be glossed
- 'It made sense that bookshop owners would also employ the four-legged security guards …' glossed by e.g. cats were then brought in to protect bookshops too
- 'Cats were easy to find' glossed by e.g. it was straightforward to come by cats OR 'all you had to do was feed them as compensation' glossed by e.g. cats don't require any special treatment/much looking after
  NB 'easy' must be glossed
- '(And once cats were invited …) they never really left.' glossed by e.g. cats stayed on in libraries/ bookshops

9. 1 mark for any one selection; 1 mark for comment.

NB do not reward a response which simply says 'it sums up the main ideas of the passage etc' unless the candidate goes on to explain what the main idea is.

Possible answers include:

- 'cats are quiet and want to be left alone'/'long for solitude' repeats the idea of e.g. 'goes right back to sleep'
- 'It began as a working relationship' repeats the idea of e.g. 'cats were trained'
- 'became something more than that'/'something deeper' repeats the idea of e.g. 'Cats held a special place in Egyptian society'
- 'became integral to the bookshop experience' repeats the idea of e.g. 'the photogenic spirit of the place' OR repeats the idea of e.g. 'Why do cats love bookshops?'/the title
- 'a small part of why…local shop (than buy online)' repeats the idea of the presence of cats in bookshops
- 'cat prowling around' repeats the idea of e.g. 'four-legged protectors'
- 'a big part of what makes these stores great'/'main attraction' repeats the idea of e.g. 'five seconds to impress him'/'apex of domesticated pets', etc.
- 'along with, you know' repeats humorous tone of paragraph one
- 'if you asked a cat' repeats the idea of e.g. 'once cats were invited into bookshops'/writer's humanisation of cats/second person address engages reader OR repeats the idea of e.g. 'Why do cats love bookshops?'/the title
- 'god-like status' repeats the idea of e.g. 'Egyptians worshipped them'/'the sort of treatment they received in the time of pharaoh'

CRITICAL READING

SECTION 1 – SCOTTISH TEXT

PART A – DRAMA – *Bold Girls* by Rona Munro

1. Any four points for 1 mark each.

   Possible answers include:

   - Nora criticises Cassie for her story telling
   - Nora bemoans the past
   - Nora is upset at the loss of her material for her soft furnishings
   - Marie reassures Nora
   - the tension between Cassie and Nora increases when Cassie does not answer Nora
   - Nora says she will secure credit under false pretences to buy new material
   - Marie warns Cassie that if she leaves, it will devastate Nora
   - Cassie says that Nora is stronger than she seems
   - Cassie threatens revenge on Deirdre
   - Marie assures Cassie that Deirdre will get her comeuppance
   - Cassie asks Marie how she remains so positive about her life
   - Cassie says she is no good

2. 1 mark for reference; 1 mark for comment (×2), for a maximum of 4 marks.

   Possible answers include:

   - repetition of "lost" suggests she really cares about it
   - repetition of "gone" suggests hopelessness
   - "Months" suggests how long she has been looking forward to this
   - "dreaming of the glow" suggests how affectionate she feels about the remnant
   - "Never" suggests her vision is unattainable
   - "lovely" suggests how she imagined the room to be as perfect as possible
   - use of short sentences suggests Nora speaks in an emotional voice
   - "And he's lost it" suggests her anger
   - use of stage direction/"Getting tearful in her turn" suggests Nora is going to cry
   - use of question suggests that she needs reassurance

3. 1 mark for reference; 1 mark for comment (×2), for a maximum of 4 marks.

   Possible answers include:

   - Nora becomes more argumentative towards Cassie "drawing herself up"/"She snatches up her drink and takes an angry gulp"
   - Cassie tries to avoid the confrontation with Nora "Cassie doesn't look at Nora"/"looking up at Nora"
   - Nora starts to become upset "She is getting tearful in her turn"
   - Nora finds Cassie's words incredulous "Nora stares at her for a moment, then she nods"

   - Marie realises that Cassie is at a crisis point and offers her more alcohol "Marie puts the gin bottle down in front of Cassie"
   - Cassie drinks quickly as she is on edge "Cassie helps herself to another drink"
   - Marie defiantly puts Michael's picture back up on the wall "... she goes and rehangs it carefully"

4. *Possible areas for comment include:*

   Extract:

   - Nora loudly criticises Cassie e.g. 'There's no end to your wild tales Cassie!'
   - Nora is assertive e.g. 'Well I'm going up the town tomorrow.'
   - Cassie threatens revenge e.g. 'There's a waitress up that club will be walking around without her hair tomorrow if I can find her.'

   Elsewhere:

   - connotations of bravery and resilience – the women exist in a harsh setting
   - connotations of risk taking behaviour (demonstrated by Cassie)
   - connotations of self-confidence
   - connotations of humour
   - the women have domestic and financial hardships to face
   - the women face harsh critics in their community

   Candidates may choose to answer in **bullet points** in this final question, or write a number of linked statements. There is **no requirement** to write a 'mini essay'.

   Up to 2 marks can be achieved for identifying elements of **commonality** as identified in the question.

   A further 2 marks can be achieved for **reference to the extract given**.

   4 additional marks can be awarded for similar references to **at least one other text/part of the text** by the writer.

   <u>In practice this means:</u>

   Identification of commonality (2) (e.g. theme, central relationship, importance of setting, use of imagery, development in characterisation, use of personal experience, use of narrative style, or any other key element...)

   From the extract:

   1 relevant reference to technique; 1 appropriate comment

   OR 1 relevant reference to idea; 1 appropriate comment

   OR 1 relevant reference to feature; 1 appropriate comment

   OR 1 relevant reference to text; 1 appropriate comment

   (maximum of 2 marks only for discussion of extract)

   from at **least one other text/part of the text:**

   as above (×2) for **up to 4 marks**

PART A – DRAMA – *Sailmaker* by Alan Spence

5. 1 mark for reference; 1 mark for comment (×2), up to a maximum of 4 marks.

   Possible answers include:

   - "Screw the heid" suggests that he is not himself
   - "ah dae ma best" suggests he recognises that he is trying to sort things out
   - "it's just…" suggests he is making excuses
   - "…" suggests unfinished explanation
   - "Hard on yer own" suggests he is struggling to cope
   - "Naw ye don't know/Naebody knows (unless they've been through it)" suggests only some people understand his current problems
   - "(Quieter)" suggests lack of confidence
   - "Comin hame's the worst/The boy's oot playin/Hoose is empty" suggests loneliness
   - "gets on top of ye" suggests being overwhelmed
   - Reference to furniture watching him suggests paranoia/lack of rational thought
   - "Maybe ah'm going aff ma heid!" suggests concern over mental health/suggests belittling his fear
   - "take a while" suggests difficulty of issue to be dealt with
   - "(take a while) tae get over it" acknowledgement that there is an issue
   - "If ah ever dae" suggests enormity of problem to be faced

6. 1 mark for reference; 1 mark for comment (×2), up to a maximum of 4 marks.

   Possible answers include:

   - "How ye doin wee yin?" suggests empathy
   - "What's this ye've got?/(Picks up yacht)" suggests he's taking an interest in Alec
   - "Ah could paint it if ye like" suggests Billy is proactive
   - "Should come up really nice" suggests optimism
   - "Ah'll take it away wi me/Get it done this week" suggests urgency
   - "Nae bother!" suggests helpfulness
   - reference to possible finished appearance of yacht suggests practical ability/skill/imagination/resourcefulness/creativity …

7. 1 mark for reference; 1 mark for comment.

   Possible answers include:

   Alec

   "It'll be dead real, eh?" suggests excitement/gratitude

   Reference to question mark suggests interest

   Davie

   "Away tae Never Never Land!" suggests sarcasm/lack of enthusiasm/dismissiveness

   Reference to exclamation mark suggests sarcasm.

8. 1 mark for each point, up to a maximum of 2 marks.

   Possible answers include:

   - Symbolises Davie's inaction
   - Symbolises Billy's action
   - represents Alec's (childhood) belief in Davie
   - symbolises Alec and Davie's relationship
   - symbolises Davie's previous trade
   - reference to colours/football associations
   - symbolises Alec's childhood
   - symbolises freedom/hope/new horizons
   - yacht represents conflict

9. Possible areas for comment include:

   Extract:

   Billy could be seen to be interfering in Davie's relationship with Alec e.g. "He'll get on a lot better if you screw the heid, right?"

   Billy shows interest in/concern for Alec e.g. "how ye doin wee yin/what's this ye've got?"

   Elsewhere:

   Billy is helpful and tries to give practical advice to Alec and to Davie (in terms of their domestic situation as well as possible employment …).

   The relationship between Billy and Ian (which is a close one) is in direct contrast to the relationship between Alec and Davie because their relationship worsens.

   The family interest in football is at the centre of many interactions between the main characters.

   There is some role reversal because Alec carries out the traditional 'adult' chores/functions. 8 Candidates may choose to answer in **bullet points** in this final question, or write a number of linked statements. There is **no requirement** to write a 'mini essay'.

   The yacht represents the breakdown of the family relationship between Alec and Davie and Billy's attempts to fix it up show that he tries to help mend the family relationship.

   Up to 2 marks can be achieved for identifying elements of **commonality** as identified in the question.

   A further 2 marks can be achieved for **reference to the extract given.**

   4 additional marks can be awarded for similar references to **at least one other text/part of the text** by the writer.

   In practice this means:

   Identification of commonality (2) (e.g. theme, central relationship, importance of setting, use of imagery, development in characterisation, use of personal experience, use of narrative style, or any other key element…)

   from the extract:

   1 × relevant reference to technique
   1 × appropriate comment

   OR 1 × relevant reference to idea
   1 × appropriate comment

   References to the past are used to contextualise current strains in the characters' relationships (e.g. death of the mother; unemployment from the sail-making trade…).

   Davie is a traditionalist, in terms of family roles/aspirations, whereas Alec breaks from these traditions (e.g. with further education).

   Family attitudes to education highlight the differences between Ian and Alec and Alec and Davie.

OR 1 × relevant reference to feature
1 × appropriate comment

OR 1 × relevant reference to text
1 × appropriate comment

(maximum of 2 marks only for discussion of extract)

from at **least one other text/part of the text:**

as above (×2) for **up to 4 marks**

PART A — DRAMA — *Tally's Blood* by Ann Marie Di Mambro

10. 1 mark for reference; 1 mark for comment (×2), up to a maximum of 4 marks.

Possible answers include:

- "You better watch these lassies" suggests warning him off
- *"(Franco scoffs)"* suggests that he is dismissive
- "Who is it anyway?" suggests loaded question
- "This is not "anybody"" suggests he is defensive
- *"(Disapproving)"* suggests critical, judgemental etc
- "What if she is?" suggests challenging statement

11. (a) 1 mark for reference; 1 mark for comment.

    Possible answers include:

    - "six or seven weans"/"*(shocked)*"/"Eight weans!" suggests her surprise at the size of the family
    - "She cannie even look after them right" suggests that she feels the family is neglected/not cared for properly
    - "It's no fair" suggests that she is jealous of Bridget's family

    (b) 1 mark for reference; 1 mark for comment.

    Possible answers include:

    - "Eight." suggests a neutral statement of fact/not critical
    - "They're a great family" suggests he has admiration for the family
    - "Really close" suggests he thinks the family have a good bond

12. 1 mark for reference; 1 mark for comment (×2), up to a maximum of 4 marks.

Possible answers include:

- "I wasn't looking" suggests he is serious about Bridget/not hoping to meet someone else
- "I told you, Rosinella, I've got someone" suggests seriousness/determination/loyalty
- "What if I am?" suggests he has his own opinions/is independent
- "You know nothing about Bridget" suggests the depth of his feelings for her
- *"(Indignant)"* suggests he can become angry/irritated
- "Good looking"/"a good kisser"/"a good dancer" suggests he is self-assured/confident
- "Oh they like that alright"/"they're all over me" suggests he is conceited
- "you've got the warm blood"/"it's one thing to play around with them" suggests prior romantic liaisons

13. Possible areas for comment include:

    Extract:

    - Rosinella shows her prejudice against Scottish girls e.g. 'These Scotch girls they're all the same.'
    - Rosinella is resentful of the fact that she has not been able to have children of her own e.g. 'Twelve years I've been married – and nothing.'

    Elsewhere:

    - Rosinella is shown as caring in that she offers Lucia a new life in Scotland
    - Rosinella is seen to spoil Lucia
    - Rosinella comes into conflict with her husband Massimo about Lucia's upbringing
    - Rosinella is proud of her Italian heritage
    - Rosinella tries to ensure that Franco and Bridget won't be together
    - Rosinella suffers (when, for example, Massimo is imprisoned)
    - Rosinella shows signs of hypocrisy over romantic relationships

    Candidates may choose to answer in **bullet points** in this final question, or write a number of linked statements. There is **no requirement** to write a 'mini essay'.

    Up to 2 marks can be achieved for identifying elements of **commonality** as identified in the question.

    A further 2 marks can be achieved for **reference to the extract given.**

    4 additional marks can be awarded for similar references to **at least one other text/part of the text** by the writer.

    In practice this means:

    Identification of commonality (2) (e.g. theme, central relationship, importance of setting, use of imagery, development in characterisation, use of personal experience, use of narrative style, or any other key element…)

    from the extract:

    1 × relevant reference to technique
    1 × appropriate comment

    OR 1 × relevant reference to idea
    1 × appropriate comment

    OR 1 × relevant reference to feature
    1 × appropriate comment

    OR 1 × relevant reference to text
    1 × appropriate comment

    (maximum of 2 marks only for discussion of extract)

    from at **least one other text/part of the text:**

    as above (×2) for **up to 4 marks**

PART B — PROSE — *The Cone-Gatherers* by Robin Jenkins

14. 1 mark for reference; 1 mark for comment (×2), up to a maximum of 4 marks.

Possible answers include:

- "Put it back, Calum," suggests Neil is in charge
- "Would it be alright if…" suggests Calum is anxious to receive permission from Neil

- "It would be stealing"/"Get your jacket...hold it in front of the fire." suggests Neil assumes parental role
- "Calum was delighted"/"I'm not telling," suggests Calum is eager to please Neil

15. 1 mark for reference; 1 mark for comment (×2), up to a maximum of 4 marks.

Possible answers include:

- "other noises outside" suggests disturbance
- "drumming of the rain" suggests ominous sound
- reference to use of colon suggests threatening noises are identified
- "dog's bark" suggests aggression
- "scratching on it as of paws" suggests fear of the unknown
- "stared towards the door" suggests fear
- "the lady cry out" suggests alarming exclamation
- "key rattled in the lock" suggests getting closer/ person outside coming in
- "The door was flung open" suggests dramatic entrance
- "loudest peal of thunder" suggests terrifying noise

16. 1 mark for reference; 1 mark for comment (×2), up to a maximum of 4 marks.

Possible answers include:

- "Neil did not know what to do or say" suggests Neil is at a loss/very confused
- "silent" suggests he doesn't know what to say
- "abjectness" suggests loss of pride
- "betrayal of himself" suggests he feels he is not giving an account of himself or Calum
- "All his vows..." suggests he feels he is going back on all his intentions/promises regarding Calum
- "rheumatism tortured him"/"fire had been pressed into..." suggests he is suffering intensely
- "punish him as he deserved" suggests he is full of self-loathing
- "He could not lift his head" suggests he is unable to face the situation
- "lifetime of frightened submissiveness" suggests he is acutely aware of his place in the 'class system'
- "Suddenly" suggests shock/surprise (that Calum is speaking)

17. Possible areas for comment include:

Extract:

- Neil's almost paternal care for Calum: e.g. "Neil went over to attend to the fire."
- Neil's acute awareness of social class/rank e.g. "A life of frightened submissiveness."
- Calum's innocence e.g. "I would put it back."

Elsewhere:

- Calum is linked with animals and nature. He is at home in the trees
- Calum is not resentful of his own appearance. This is in direct contrast with Duror's view
- Calum is generally seen to represent innocence

- Neil makes sacrifices in order to care for his brother
- Neil has a rational view of the world and is less interested in nature than Calum
- Neil believes the war will be beneficial to people like him

Candidates may choose to answer in **bullet points** in this final question, or write a number of linked statements. There is **no requirement** to write a 'mini essay'.

Up to 2 marks can be achieved for identifying elements of **commonality** as identified in the question.

A further 2 marks can be achieved for **reference to the extract given.**

4 additional marks can be awarded for similar references to **at least one other text/part of the text** by the writer.

<u>In practice this means:</u>

Identification of commonality (2) (e.g. theme, central relationship, importance of setting, use of imagery, development in characterisation, use of personal experience, use of narrative style, or any other key element...)

From the extract:

1 × relevant reference to technique
1 × appropriate comment

OR 1 × relevant reference to idea

1 × appropriate comment

OR 1 × relevant reference to feature
1 × appropriate comment

OR 1 × relevant reference to text
1 × appropriate comment

(maximum of 2 marks only for discussion of extract)

from at **least one other text/part of the text:**

as above (×2) for **up to 4 marks**

PART B — PROSE — *The Testament of Gideon Mack* **by James Robertson**

18. 1 mark for reference; 1 mark for comment (×2), up to a maximum of 4 marks.

Possible answers include:

- short first sentence is dramatic
- "sweating" suggests nervousness
- "seething" suggests intensity
- "wrecked" suggests overcome with anxiety
- "afraid" suggests anxiety
- "provoked" suggests disturbed
- "crisis" suggests importance of situation
- "I paced ..." suggests stress
- "as if in contact with an electric fence" suggesting agitation
- contradiction in wanting to go but afraid to suggests indecision
- "(I paced ...) in and out of every room, up and down the stairs" suggests incessant walking, restlessness etc
- says he wants to go for a run "to calm down" suggests he is in a heightened state

19. 1 mark for reference; 1 mark for comment.

Possible answers include:

- "I've had a good look round." suggests enthusiasm
- "Is this an awkward moment?" suggests sensitivity/ social awareness
- "You wouldn't like to come for a walk instead?" suggests persistence
- "I can't say I understood everything" suggests modesty
- "it was quite thought-provoking" suggests intellectual curiosity
- "while I was looking down through that window" suggests nosiness

20. 1 mark for each point, up to a maximum of 2 marks.

Possible answers include:

- he sees it as fate/the influence of the Stone
- going there will allow him to discuss things with her
- if she saw the Stone, he would talk to John and Elsie
- if she didn't see the Stone, he would admit madness or a breakdown and seek help

21. 1 mark for reference; 1 mark for comment (×2), up to a maximum of 4 marks.

Possible answers include:

- "I wouldn't be back (for nearly a week)" suggests longer than anticipated absence
- "Nor could I have foreseen" suggests mysterious event
- "utterly transformed" suggests unexpectedly huge change
- "Nor indeed...could I have guessed" suggests complete surprise
- repetition of "Nor" emphasises his uncertainty
- "but her dog" suggests suspense/anticipation

22. Possible areas for comment include:

Extract:

Reference made to curiosity about Keldo woods and the cave at the Black Jaws, e.g. "take her to Keldo woods, and show her the Stone."

Elsewhere:

- the manse at Ochtermill, linked to Gideon's origins, his early family influences, and the theme of religion
- Keldo woods, linked with the supernatural, local superstitions, and Gideon's 'inner life'/psychology, etc.
- the Black Jaws, linked with Gideon's transformational meeting with the Devil

Candidates may choose to answer in **bullet points** in this final question, or write a number of linked statements. There is **no requirement** to write a 'mini essay'.

Up to 2 marks can be achieved for identifying elements of **commonality** as identified in the question.

A further 2 marks can be achieved for **reference to the extract given.**

4 additional marks can be awarded for similar references to **at least one other text/part of the text** by the writer.

In practice this means:

Identification of commonality (2) (e.g. theme, central relationship, importance of setting, use of imagery, development in characterisation, use of personal experience, use of narrative style, or any other key element...)

From the extract:

1 × relevant reference to technique
1 × appropriate comment

OR 1 × relevant reference to idea
1 × appropriate comment

OR 1 × relevant reference to feature
1 × appropriate comment

OR 1 × relevant reference to text
1 × appropriate comment

(maximum of 2 marks only for discussion of extract)

from at **least one other text/part of the text:**

as above (× 2) for **up to 4 marks**

PART B — PROSE — *Kidnapped* by Robert Louis Stevenson

23. 1 mark for reference; 1 mark for comment (×2), up to a maximum of 4 marks.

Possible answers include:

- "he could bear it no longer" suggests that there has been previous tension
- "this is no way for two friends (to take a small accident)" suggests there has been a difference of opinion
- "I'm sorry" suggests remorse
- "ye'd better say it" suggests threatening/challenging comment
- "I have nothing" denial suggests something unsaid
- "disconcerted" suggests flustered
- "I was meanly pleased" suggests David is enjoying Alan's discomfort
- "of course, ye were to blame" suggests David thinks Alan was at fault
- "coolly" suggests tense atmosphere between the pair

24. 1 mark for reference; 1 mark for comment (×2), up to a maximum of 4 marks.

Possible answers include:

- "This pierced me like a sword" suggests that he was wounded/really hurt
- "lay bare" suggests vulnerability
- "I cried" suggests strong emotion
- "Do you think I am one to turn my back..." suggests he is indignant
- "cast it up to me" suggest defensiveness
- repetition of the word "you" suggests frustration

25. 1 mark for reference; 1 mark for comment (×2), up to a maximum of 4 marks.

Possible answers include:

- appropriate reference conciliatory
- appropriate reference worried

- appropriate reference guilty conscience
- appropriate reference concerned
- appropriate reference manipulative

26. Possible areas for comment include:

Extract:

Example of friendship being strained in the extract, but at the same time we can see their genuine caring heart of their friendship for each other amidst the strained atmosphere, e.g. "This pierced me like a sword"

Elsewhere:

- Alan & David's friendship is surprising as they come from opposite political backgrounds and beliefs
- their friendship is challenged throughout the novel
- friendship established when David overhears crew of *Covenant* planning to overthrow Alan Breck and David warns Alan
- violent fight in the Round-House of the Covenant is where David helps Alan
- Alan gives David a silver button as a token of gratitude/friendship for David's actions
- murder of Red Fox puts grave doubts in David's head about Alan's character and their continuing friendship
- Alan and David continue on their journey and therefore their friendship is maintained
- Alan loses all their money at a game of cards and this puts pressure on their friendship
- David challenges Alan to a duel – Alan refuses and they make up
- when they arrive in Edinburgh, Alan helps David gain his rightful title and inheritance
- with the help of Rankeillor, David gives Alan money to get back to France
- David and Alan, at the end of the novel, struggle to part due to their strong friendship

Candidates may choose to answer in **bullet points** in this final question, or write a number of linked statements. There is **no requirement** to write a 'mini essay'.

Up to 2 marks can be achieved for identifying elements of **commonality** as identified in the question.

A further 2 marks can be achieved for **reference to the extract given.**

4 additional marks can be awarded for similar references to **at least one other text/part of the text** by the writer.

In practice this means:

Identification of commonality (2) (e.g. theme, central relationship, importance of setting, use of imagery, development in characterisation, use of personal experience, use of narrative style, or any other key element...)

from the extract:

1 × relevant reference to technique
1 × appropriate comment

OR 1 × relevant reference to idea
1 × appropriate comment

OR 1 × relevant reference to feature
1 × appropriate comment

OR 1 × relevant reference to text
1 × appropriate comment

(maximum of 2 marks only for discussion of extract)

from at **least one other text/part of the text:**

as above (×2) for **up to 4 marks**

PART B – PROSE – *The Red Door* by Iain Crichton Smith

27. 1 mark for reference; 1 mark for comment (×2), up to a maximum of 4 marks.

Possible answers include:

- "stared" suggests he can't make sense of it
- "deep caves" suggests the unknown
- "seemed to be drawn inside it" suggests the door has almost supernatural power
- "veins and passages" suggests hidden parts/secrets
- "magic (door)" suggests it is irrational/unexpected/ unexplained/impressive
- "deep red light" suggests unexpected brightness/ intense colour
- "appear alive" suggests door has life of its own
- "very odd and very puzzling" suggests lack of explanation
- "scratching his head" suggests confusion caused by the door
- "couldn't see himself in it" suggests unnatural quality
- "sucked into it" suggests odd power/attraction
- "different" suggests stands out

28. One mark for each point.

Possible answers include:

- he loves the door
- he is not annoyed that it has been painted
- he is impressed by (the idea of) the door

29. 1 mark for reference; 1 mark for comment.

Possible answers include:

- "childlikeness" suggests the beginning of a life/sense of wonder
- "stirring within him" suggests new birth/emergence
- "rousing" suggests awakening/change
- "new day" suggests a beginning
- "joyously" suggests excitement (at new beginning)
- "early" suggests the beginning of a journey

30. 1 mark for reference; 1 mark for comment (×2), up to a maximum of 4 marks.

Possible answers include:

- "sparkling frost" suggests attractive, magical, appealing surroundings
- "new" suggests freshness
- "diamonds" suggests something precious
- "glittered" suggests attractive/appealing

- "millions of them" suggests abundance
- "shone bravely" suggests having an admirable quality
- "pride" suggests pleased with what it has achieved
- "spirit" suggests enthusiasm/energy
- "emerged" suggests birth/renewal
- "brightly" suggests fresh/appealing
- "let me live my own life" suggests independence/aspiration

31. Possible areas for comment include:

Extract:

Themes from extract e.g.

Individual vs conformity, restrictive nature of community/environment.

Elsewhere:

- *Mother and Son*
  themes of freedom/lack of freedom/restrictive nature of mother and son relationship
- *The Telegram*
  themes of restrictive nature of small town community – treatment of the 'thin woman,' intrusive/restrictive nature of the community as a group
- *The Painter*
  themes of restrictive nature of community – William has to escape the community to gain freedom/creativity
- *In Church*
  Lack of freedom/entrapment caused by war. Candidates may choose to answer in **bullet points** in this final question, or write a number of linked statements. There is **no requirement** to write a 'mini essay'

Up to 2 marks can be achieved for identifying elements of **commonality** as identified in the question.

A further 2 marks can be achieved for **reference to the extract given.**

4 additional marks can be awarded for similar references to **at least one other text/part of the text** by the writer.

In practice this means:

Identification of commonality (2) (e.g. theme, central relationship, importance of setting, use of imagery, development in characterisation, use of personal experience, use of narrative style, or any other key element...)

From the extract:

1 × relevant reference to technique
1 × appropriate comment

OR 1 × relevant reference to idea
1 × appropriate comment

OR 1 × relevant reference to feature
1 × appropriate comment

OR 1 × relevant reference to text
1 × appropriate comment

(maximum of 2 marks only for discussion of extract)

from at **least one other text/part of the text:**

as above (×2) for **up to 4 marks**

PART B – PROSE – *Away in a Manger* by Anne Donovan

32. 1 mark for reference; 1 mark for comment.

Possible answers include:

- "Are you cauld?" suggests a reason to postpone trip
- "A vision of warmth"/"a fire"/"a mug of hot tea" suggests more attractive options
- "We could come back"/"another night" suggest an attempt to cancel/postpone trip
- "Naw, Mammy, naw"/"we cannae go hame noo"/"we're nearly there"/"you promised" suggests Amy senses Sandra's reluctance
- "All right, we'll go." suggests giving in, but not keen

33. 1 mark for reference; 1 mark for comment (×2), up to a maximum of 4 marks.

Possible answers include:

- "gaun on aboot the lights (for weeks)" suggests Sandra is tired of hearing about the decorations, etc
- "ower and done wi" suggests she wants the season to be finished
- "she was sick of it all" suggests that was bored/weary with the season
- "opened longer and longer" suggests she is tired of her shop's extended opening hours
- "trippin ower wan another" suggests she hates the busy shops/festive season crowds
- "everybody in a bad mood" suggests she hates the collective misery
- "trachled (wi parcels)" suggests she dislikes the exhaustion of Christmas shopping
- "those bloody Christmas records" suggests she dislikes the seasonal music
- "extra hours"/"old bag of a supervisor"/"extra couple of hours"/"hit her ower the heid..." suggest she doesn't like the additional work pressures that the season brings

34. 1 mark for each point.

Possible answers include:

- wants to please her (by taking her to see the decorations)
- cares about her appearance (by buying her nice clothes)
- wants the best for her
- she is full of admiration for the way she looks
- cares about her manners, etc.

35. 1 mark for reference; 1 mark for comment (×2), up to a maximum of 4 marks.

Possible answers include:

- "the cauld evaporated" suggests the cold (magically) seems to disappear
- "shimmerin wi light" suggests twinkling/sparkling effect
- "brightness sharp" suggests intense glow
- "brightness sharp against the gloomy street" suggests light/dark contrast
- "Trees frosted wi light" suggests a silvery glow to the surroundings

- "Lights shaped intae circles and flowers" suggests fantasy-inspired decorations
- "plastic jewellery sets wee lassies love" suggests appealing to children
- "mad rhythm" suggests 'unreal' quality
- "all bleezin wi light" suggests incredibly bright
- "(Amy gazed at them,) eyes shinin" suggests wonder

36. Possible areas for comment include:

Extract:

Reference to main theme of extract e.g. Mother/ daughter relationship.

Elsewhere:

- *All that Glisters*
  exploration of relationship between main character and father (who has died), also between main character and mother and auntie
- *Dear Santa*
  exploration of mother daughter relationships (daughter narrates)
- *Zimmerobics*
  exploration of relationship between Miss Knight and her niece Catherine (also with Cheryl from Zimmerobics class)
- *Virtual Pals*
  exploration of the virtual relationship between Siobhan and Irina
- *A Chitterin' Bite*
  exploration between main character and childhood friend, and main character with adult lover

Candidates may choose to answer in **bullet points** in this final question, or write a number of linked statements. There is **no requirement** to write a 'mini essay'.

Up to 2 marks can be achieved for identifying elements of **commonality** as identified in the question.

A further 2 marks can be achieved for **reference to the extract given.**

4 additional marks can be awarded for similar references to **at least one other text/part of the text** by the writer.

<u>In practice this means:</u>

Identification of commonality (2) (e.g. theme, central relationship, importance of setting, use of imagery, development in characterisation, use of personal experience, use of narrative style, or any other key element...)

From the extract:

1 × relevant reference to technique
1 × appropriate comment

OR 1 × relevant reference to idea
1 × appropriate comment

OR 1 × relevant reference to feature
1 × appropriate comment

OR 1 × relevant reference to text
1 × appropriate comment

(maximum of 2 marks only for discussion of extract)

from at **least one other text/part of the text:**

as above (×2) for **up to 4 marks**

PART C — POETRY — *Mrs Midas* by Carol Ann Duffy

37. 1 mark for reference; 1 mark for comment (×2), up to a maximum of 4 marks.

Possible answers include:

- "glass of wine" suggests leisure time
- "unwind" suggests away from stresses
  NB. Do not accept 'relaxed' as the comment as this is a lift
- "while the vegetables cooked" suggests time to yourself/job done
- "relaxed" suggests taking it easy
- "gently" suggests peaceful/leisurely
- "snapping a twig" suggests something ordinary/ harmless/non-threatening

38. 1 mark for reference; 1 mark for comment (×2), up to a maximum of 4 marks.

Possible answers include:

- "(the garden) was long" suggests too far away to see clearly
- "visibility poor" vision impaired by the conditions
- "dark" not enough light to see
- "seems" suggests that she is not sure
- "drink the light of the sky" suggests there is not enough natural light to make out what's happening
- "but that..." suggests speaker is trying to make sense of what she has seen
- "that twig in his hand was gold" suggests speaker is struggling to make sense of incongruity
- "sat in his palm like a light bulb" suggests speaker is searching for comparisons to explain what she has seen
- "On."/reference to short single word sentence suggests surprise
- "is he putting fairy lights in the tree?"/reference to the question suggests speaker is searching for an explanation

39. 1 mark for reference; 1 mark for comment (×2), up to a maximum of 4 marks.

Possible answers include:

- "He came into the house."/"The doorknobs gleamed."/"He drew the blinds."/reference to short sentences suggests something significant is taking place
- "doorknobs gleamed" suggests unusual/note-worthy shine
- "He sat in that chair like a king" suggests incongruity
- "burnished throne" suggests the chair is transformed/striking
- "strange" suggests out of the ordinary
- "wild" suggests out of control
- "vain" suggests pride/self-important, etc.
- "What in the name of God is going on?"/reference to question suggests an inexplicable/startling event
- "He started to laugh" suggests unsettling reaction

- "Within seconds" suggests things happening rapidly
- "spitting out" suggests violent action
- "corn on the cob into teeth of the rich" suggests rapid transformation of meal into gold
- "toyed" suggests menace/taking pleasure
- "shaking hand" suggests nervousness
- "glass, goblet, golden chalice" disbelief at transformation

40. Possible areas for comment include:

Extract:

Reference to creation of interesting characters in the extract e.g. Mrs Midas – her life being turned upside down by the changes in her husband. Candidates could equally concentrate on changes within Mr Midas.

Elsewhere:

- *War Photographer*
  the character of the war photographer – how he is affected by the things he has seen, and how his work takes him into places which contrast starkly with his home and home country
- *Valentine*
  character displays an 'unusual' take on/attitude to love
- *Havisham*
  character displays ambivalent, and at times hostile, attitude to her ex-lover
- *Anne Hathaway*
  character displays a clear sense of the loss she feels at the memory of her husband
- *Originally*
  Character shows a clear sense of shock brought on by the house-moving. Character struggles with identity

Candidates may choose to answer in **bullet points** in this final question, or write a number of linked statements. There is **no requirement** to write a 'mini essay'.

Up to 2 marks can be achieved for identifying elements of **commonality** as identified in the question.

A further 2 marks can be achieved for **reference to the extract given**.

4 additional marks can be awarded for similar references to **at least one other part of the text** by the writer.

In practice this means:

Identification of commonality (2) (e.g. theme, central relationship, importance of setting, use of imagery, development in characterisation, use of personal experience, use of narrative style, or any other key element…)

From the extract:

1 × relevant reference to technique
1 × appropriate comment

OR 1 × relevant reference to idea
1 × appropriate comment

OR 1 × relevant reference to feature
1 × appropriate comment

OR 1 × relevant reference to text
1 × appropriate comment

(maximum of 2 marks only for discussion of extract)

from at **least one other text/part of the text:**

as above (×2) for **up to 4 marks**

PART C — POETRY — *Slate* by Edwin Morgan

41. 1 mark for reference; 1 mark for comment (×2), up to a maximum of 4 marks.

Possible answers include:

- "saw Lewis laid down" suggests the island of Lewis was placed there as if it was a small, light thing

  OR

- personification of Lewis suggests the deliberate force of the island's formation
- "thunder" suggests noise/danger/drama
- "volcanic fires" suggests the destructive force/massive elemental force
- "watched long seas plunder faults" suggests the seas were like an army attacking
- "Staffa cooled" suggests the island had to recover from the heat of its formation
- "Drumlins blue as bruises" suggests the hills have been attacked and left hurt/the violent power/aggression of the formation
- "grated off like nutmegs" suggests the hills were tiny and no match compared to the power of their creator

42. 1 mark for reference; 1 mark for comment (×2), up to a maximum of 4 marks.

Possible answers include:

- "a great glen" suggests the size/magnificence of the glen running across the island
- "a rough back" suggests the island has a tough, resilient protective layer
- "the ages must streak" suggests time will leave a lasting mark
- "surely strike" suggests the island will be attacked as time goes on
- "seldom stroke" suggests the island will rarely be treated kindly
- "raised and shaken" suggests the island will endure despite being treated harshly
- "tens of thousands of rains" highlights the prevalence of rain
- "blizzards" shows the violence of the storms
- "sea-poundings" suggests the sea beat the land
- "shouldered off" suggests the island is able to shrug off these elements/not be beaten by them

43. 1 mark for reference; 1 mark for comment (×2), up to a maximum of 4 marks.

Possible answers include:

- use of two short sentences/contrast of short sentences with previous long sentence highlights the arrival of humans
- positioning of exclamation mark draws our attention to the transition
- "Memory of men!"/"that was to come" suggests the evolving use of the landscape
- "empty hunger"/"threw walls to the sky" personifies the landscape as being eager for something new
- "the sorry glory of a rainbow"/oxymoron highlights the empty and brief beauty of a rainbow compared to the enduring nature of the landscape/the island

- "rainbow" suggests new beginning/hope/new start/ diversity
- "Their heels kicked" suggests impatience for something to happen
- "flint, chalk, slate"/list suggests progression over time

44. Possible areas for comment include:

Extract: Themes of change, new beginnings, vision of Scotland, violence/brutality of nature, hostile environment.

Elsewhere:

- *In the Snack-bar*
  theme of society being uncaring, hostile or challenging environment
- *Hyena*
  theme of the brutality of nature, hostile/challenging environment
- *Trio*
  theme of humanism versus religion, idea of hope/ new beginnings
- *Good Friday*
  theme of religion or social class, challenging environment
- *Winter*
  theme of death, challenging environment

Candidates may choose to answer in **bullet points** in this final question, or write a number of linked statements. There is **no requirement** to write a 'mini essay'.

Up to 2 marks can be achieved for identifying elements of **commonality** as identified in the question.

A further 2 marks can be achieved for **reference to the extract given.**

4 additional marks can be awarded for similar references to **at least one other text/part of the text by the writer.**

In practice this means:

Identification of commonality (2) (e.g. theme, central relationship, importance of setting, use of imagery, development in characterisation, use of personal experience, use of narrative style, or any other key element...)

From the extract:

1 × relevant reference to technique
1 × appropriate comment

OR 1 × relevant reference to idea
1 × appropriate comment

OR 1 × relevant reference to feature
1 × appropriate comment

OR 1 × relevant reference to text
1 × appropriate comment

(maximum of 2 marks only for discussion of extract)

from at **least one other text/part of the text:**

as above (× 2) for up to **4 marks**

PART C — POETRY — *Memorial* by Norman MacCaig

45. 1 mark for each point, up to a maximum of 2 marks.

Possible answers include:

- he no longer feels enjoyment
- her death is with him at all times in all places

- her death interrupts everything
- her death restricts his ability to communicate
- he cannot get close to other people/another person
- she still seems to influence him
- he feels isolated/apart from her

46. 1 mark for reference; 1 mark for comment (×2), up to a maximum of 4 marks.

Possible answers include:

- repetition of "Everywhere" emphasises omnipresence of her death
- repetition of "no" emphasises there is no escape from the fact of her death
- contrast of "silence" and "carousel" suggests the removal of joy from his life
- "it's a web" feels restricted or trapped
- "How can my hand clasp ..." suggests that loved one is irreplaceable
- reference to question suggests he can't find answers/ no closure
- "Thick (death)" suggests the heavy weight of her death enveloping him
- "intolerable" hard to bear
- "distance" suggests isolation/loneliness following death, etc.

47. 1 mark for reference; 1 mark for comment (×2), up to a maximum of 4 marks.

Possible answers include:

- "She grieves for my grief" she appears to share his emotions/emotional reactions
- "she tells me" she still communicates with him
- "(her dying) shapes my mind" continued influence
- "But I hear" suggests continued presence
- use of present tense suggests continued closeness
- repetition of words suggests her voice still seems to be there

48. 1 mark for reference; 1 mark for comment.

Possible answers include:

- expression from ending
- linked reference/idea from elsewhere
  NB The linked reference may be to the poem as a whole
- "elegy" relates to the form of the poem
- "walking" refers back to idea of "Everywhere I go"
- "masterpiece" refers back to idea of "carved more gently"
- "true fiction" refers back to idea of "black words"
- "ugliness of death" refers back to idea of "thick death"/death is mentioned many times in the poem
- "I am her sad music" refers back to idea of "sound of soundlessness" etc

49. Possible areas for comment include:

Extract:

Reference to use of language exploring experiences of death and loss.

Elsewhere:

- *Basking Shark*
  description of the encounter with the shark, and how it caused the poet to think/reflect on how he viewed man/nature, etc.

- *Visiting Hour*
  language reflects the difficulty of dealing with feelings/making sense of highly charged emotional experience

- *Assisi*
  language reflects important discoveries about how society/the church treats disabled/vulnerable/poor people

- *Aunt Julia*
  language concentrates on discovery of the importance of the past/people from the past/people who are no longer with us. Importance of/remoteness of other cultures

- *Sounds of the day*
  word choice/imagery reflects the lasting effects/impact of the parting.

Candidates may choose to answer in **bullet points** in this final question, or write a number of linked statements. There is **no requirement** to write a 'mini essay'.

Up to 2 marks can be achieved for identifying elements of **commonality** as identified in the question.

A further 2 marks can be achieved for **reference to the extract given.**

4 additional marks can be awarded for similar references to **at least one other part of the text** by the writer.

<u>In practice this means:</u>

Identification of commonality (2) (e.g. theme, central relationship, importance of setting, use of imagery, development in characterisation, use of personal experience, use of narrative style, or any other key element...)

From the extract:

1 × relevant reference to technique
1 × appropriate comment

OR 1 × relevant reference to idea
1 × appropriate comment

OR 1 × relevant reference to feature
1 × appropriate comment

OR 1 × relevant reference to text
1 × appropriate comment

(maximum of 2 marks only for discussion of extract)

from at **least one other text/part of the text:**

as above (×2) for **up to 4 marks**

PART C — POETRY — *Gap Year* by Jackie Kay

50. 1 mark for reference; 1 mark for comment.

Possible answers include:

- "I'd stare" suggests intense interest

- "for days"/"weeks" suggests interest so great it was maintained over a period of time

- "willing you" suggests sense of anticipation

- "hardly able to believe" suggests can't comprehend the enormity of the event

- "real baby" suggests the reality is momentous

51. 1 mark for reference; 1 mark for comment (×2), up to a maximum of 4 marks.

Possible answers include:

- "I'd feel the mound" suggests physical closeness

- "foot against my heart" suggests extreme closeness

- "I imagined I felt you laugh" suggests absorption in the experience

- "I'd play you … (music)" suggests a sense of nurture

- "I'd talk to you" suggests communication

- "my close stranger" suggests early intimacy

- "Tumshie" suggests playful nickname

- "ask when you were coming to meet me" suggests excitement/anticipation

52. (a) 1 mark for reference; 1 mark for comment (×2), up to a maximum of 4 marks.

Possible answers include:

- "stare at your bed" indicates she is missing her son

- "Your handsome face" indicates a sense of pride

- repetition of "away" suggests isolation/distance between them

- the many references to different places "Costa Rica … Machu Picchu", etc. indicates wonderment at the scale of the trip

- "I follow your trails" indicates absorption

- the use of "from … to" structure indicates admiration for the distance travelled

- references to time "Now … then … yesterday" indicate admiration for the length of the trip

- references to "photograph/web cam" indicate pride that the trip is being documented

- "your face is grainy, blurry" reiterates the distance between them

(b) 1 mark for reference; 1 mark for comment.

Possible answers include:

- "Have you considered" indicates realism/lack of romance/implied criticism of mother

- "altitude sickness" indicates warning of potential danger

- "Christ" indicates exasperation/disapproval

- "sixteen thousand feet above sea level" reiterates remoteness/danger/hostile environment

53. Possible areas for comment include:

Extract:

Reference to bedroom at home or a destination (Costa Rica, Peru, Bolivia) – comment might include mention of themes of isolation, loss, separation, growing up, family relationships, identity, or could focus on character and/or character relationships.

Elsewhere:

- *Keeping Orchids*
  settings of home and train station leading to comments on – family relationships, sense of identity, characters of mother and daughter, etc.

- *Lucozade*
  hospital setting leading to comments on – family relationships, sense of identity, loss, separation, etc.

- *My grandmother's Houses*
  settings of old home, new home, cleaning house leading to comments on – family relationships, identity, etc.

- *Bed*
  hospital setting leading to comments on – family relationships, isolation, separation, etc.

Candidates may choose to answer in **bullet points** in this final question, or write a number of linked statements. There is **no requirement** to write a 'mini essay'.

Up to 2 marks can be achieved for identifying elements of commonality as requested in the question.

A further 2 marks can be achieved for **reference to the extract given.**

4 additional marks can be awarded for similar references to **at least one other part of the text.**

<u>In practice this means:</u>

Identification of commonality (2) (e.g. theme, central relationship, importance of setting, use of imagery, development in characterisation, use of personal experience, use of narrative style or any other key element...)

From the extract:

1 × relevant reference to technique **1** × appropriate comment

OR 1 × relevant reference to idea **1** × appropriate comment
OR 1 × relevant reference to feature **1** × appropriate comment

OR 1 × relevant reference to text **1** × appropriate comment

(maximum of 2 marks only for discussion of extract)

from at **least one other part of the text:**

as above (×2) for **up to 4 marks**

SECTION 2 – CRITICAL ESSAY

Please see the assessment criteria for the Critical Essay on page 123.

Acknowledgements

Permission has been sought from all relevant copyright holders and Hodder Gibson is grateful for the use of the following:

The article 'Can Idina Menzel ever Let It Go?' by Ed Potton © The Times/News Licensing, 6 February 2015 (2016 Reading for Understanding, Analysis and Evaluation pages 2 & 3);
An extract from 'Bold Girls' copyright © 1991 Rona Munro. Excerpted with permission of Nick Hern Books Ltd: www.nickhernbooks.co.uk (2016 Critical Reading pages 2 & 3);
An extract from 'Sailmaker' by Alan Spence. Reproduced by permission of Hodder Education (2016 Critical Reading pages 4 & 5);
An extract from 'Tally's Blood' by Ann Marie di Mambro, published by Education Scotland. Reprinted by permission of Ann Marie di Mambro/MacFarlane Chard Associates (2016 Critical Reading pages 6 & 7);
An extract from 'The Cone-Gatherers' by Robin Jenkins, published by Canongate Books Ltd. (2016 Critical Reading page 8);
An extract from 'The Testament Of Gideon Mack' by James Robertson (Hamish Hamilton 2006, Penguin Books 2007). Copyright © James Robertson, 2006. Reproduced by permission of Penguin Books Ltd. (2016 Critical Reading page 10);
An extract from 'Kidnapped' by Robert Louis Stevenson, published by Cassell and Company Ltd 1886. Public domain (2016 Critical Reading page 12);
An extract from 'The Painter' by Iain Crichton Smith, taken from 'The Red Door: The Complete English Stories 1949–76', published by Birlinn. Reproduced with permission of Birlinn Limited via PLSclear (2016 Critical Reading page 14);
An extract from 'Dear Santa' by Anne Donovan, taken from 'Hieroglyphics and Other Stories', published by Canongate Books Ltd. (2016 Critical Reading pages 16 & 17);
The poem 'Originally' by Carol Ann Duffy from 'The Other Country'. Published by Anvil Press Poetry, 1990. Copyright © Carol Ann Duffy. Reproduced by permission of the author c/o Rogers, Coleridge & White Ltd., 20 Powis Mews, London W11 1JN (2016 Critical Reading page 18);
The poem 'Good Friday' by Edwin Morgan, taken from 'New Selected Poems', published by Carcanet Press Limited 2000 (2016 Critical Reading page 20);
The poem 'Sounds of the Day' by Norman MacCaig, taken from 'The Many Days: Selected Poems of Norman MacCaig' edited by Roderick Watson, published by Polygon. Reproduced with permission of Birlinn Limited via PLSclear (2016 Critical Reading page 22);
The poem 'Keeping Orchids' by Jackie Kay, taken from 'Darling: New & Selected Poems' (Bloodaxe Books, 2007). Reproduced with permission of Bloodaxe Books. www.bloodaxebooks.com (2016 Critical Reading page 24);
'Resilience' is adapted from the article 'We must dare to dream but life is too precious to be derailed by failure' by Matthew Syed © The Times/News Licensing, 19 January 2015 (2017 Reading for Understanding, Analysis and Evaluation pages 2 & 3);
An extract from 'Bold Girls' copyright © 1991 Rona Munro. Excerpted with permission of Nick Hern Books Ltd: www.nickhernbooks.co.uk (2017 Critical Reading pages 2 & 3);
An extract from 'Sailmaker' by Alan Spence. Reproduced by permission of Hodder Education (2017 Critical Reading pages 4 & 5);
An extract from 'Tally's Blood' by Ann Marie di Mambro, published by Education Scotland. Reprinted by permission of Ann Marie di Mambro/MacFarlane Chard Associates (2017 Critical Reading pages 6 & 7);
An extract from 'The Cone-Gatherers' by Robin Jenkins, published by Canongate Books Ltd. (2017 Critical Reading page 8);
An extract from 'The Testament Of Gideon Mack' by James Robertson (Hamish Hamilton 2006, Penguin Books 2007). Copyright © James Robertson, 2006. Reproduced by permission of Penguin Books Ltd. (2017 Critical Reading page 10);
An extract from 'Kidnapped' by Robert Louis Stevenson, published by Cassell and Company Ltd 1886. Public domain (2017 Critical Reading page 12);
An extract from 'The Crater' by Iain Crichton Smith, taken from 'The Red Door: The Complete English Stories 1949–76', published by Birlinn. Reproduced with permission of Birlinn Limited via PLSclear (2017 Critical Reading page 14);
An extract from 'Zimmerobics' by Anne Donovan, taken from 'Hieroglyphics and Other Stories', published by Canongate Books Ltd. (2017 Critical Reading page 16);
The poem 'War Photographer' from 'Standing Female Nude' by Carol Ann Duffy. Published by Anvil Press Poetry, 1985. Copyright © Carol Ann Duffy. Reproduced by permission of the author c/o Rogers, Coleridge & White Ltd., 20 Powis Mews, London W11 1JN (2017 Critical Reading page 18);
The poem 'Trio' by Edwin Morgan, taken from 'New Selected Poems', published by Carcanet Press Limited 2000 (2017 Critical Reading page 20);
The poem 'Aunt Julia' by Norman MacCaig, taken from 'The Poems of Norman MacCaig' edited by Ewan McCaig, published by Polygon. Reproduced with permission of Birlinn Limited via PLSclear (2017 Critical Reading page 22);
The poem 'Bed' by Jackie Kay, taken from 'Darling: New & Selected Poems' (Bloodaxe Books, 2007). Reproduced with permission of Bloodaxe Books. www.bloodaxebooks.com (2017 Critical Reading page 24);
The article 'Why do cats love bookshops?' by Jason Diamond, taken from Literary Hub, 11 April 2016 (http://lithub.com/why-do-cats-love-bookstores/). Reproduced by permission of Jason Diamond (2018 Reading for Understanding, Analysis and Evaluation pages 2 & 3);
An extract from 'Bold Girls' copyright © 1991 Rona Munro. Excerpted with permission of Nick Hern Books Ltd: www.nickhernbooks.co.uk (2018 Critical Reading pages 2 & 3);
An extract from 'Sailmaker' by Alan Spence. Reproduced by permission of Hodder Education (2018 Critical Reading pages 4 & 5);
An extract from 'Tally's Blood' by Ann Marie di Mambro, published by Education Scotland. Reprinted by permission of Ann Marie di Mambro/MacFarlane Chard Associates (2018 Critical Reading pages 6 & 7);
An extract from 'The Cone-Gatherers' by Robin Jenkins, published by Canongate Books Ltd. (2018 Critical Reading pages 8 & 9);
An extract from 'The Testament Of Gideon Mack' by James Robertson (Hamish Hamilton 2006, Penguin Books 2007). Copyright © James Robertson, 2006. Reproduced by permission of Penguin Books Ltd. (2018 Critical Reading pages 10 & 11);
An extract from 'Kidnapped' by Robert Louis Stevenson, published by Cassell and Company Ltd 1886. Public domain (2018 Critical Reading pages 12 & 13);
An extract from 'The Red Door' by Iain Crichton Smith, taken from 'The Red Door: The Complete English Stories 1949–76', published by Birlinn. Reproduced with permission of Birlinn Limited via PLSclear (2018 Critical Reading page 14);
An extract from 'Away in a Manger' by Anne Donovan, taken from 'Hieroglyphics and Other Stories', published by Canongate Books Ltd. (2018 Critical Reading page 16);
The poem 'Mrs Midas' from 'The Other Country' by Carol Ann Duffy. Published by Anvil Press Poetry, 1990. Copyright © Carol Ann Duffy. Reproduced by permission of the author c/o Rogers, Coleridge & White Ltd., 20 Powis Mews, London W11 1JN (2018 Critical Reading page 18);
The poem 'Slate' by Edwin Morgan, taken from 'Collected Poems', published by Carcanet Press Limited 1990 (2018 Critical Reading page 20);
The poem 'Memorial' by Norman MacCaig, taken from 'The Poems of Norman MacCaig' edited by Ewan McCaig, published by Polygon. Reproduced with permission of Birlinn Limited via PLSclear (2018 Critical Reading page 22);
The poem 'Gap Year' by Jackie Kay, taken from 'Darling: New & Selected Poems' (Bloodaxe Books, 2007). Reproduced with permission of Bloodaxe Books. www.bloodaxebooks.com (2018 Critical Reading page 24).